PIONEERING SPIRIT
Chronicles of Evangel College's First 25 Years
1955-1980

Endorsements

Dr. Hector Cruz has done Evangel University a remarkable service in his history of the university since its founding days. I know this story well, having written a book on Evangel's historical roots that date back to the early 20th century and led to its 1955 founding. Taking the baton from where I left off, Dr. Cruz has chronicled Evangel through a book well-researched, thoughtfully written and filled with lessons that transcend this one institution. As you read these pages, you will grasp not only a deeper appreciation for Evangel's leaders over the past 70 years through thick and thin, but you will draw from this historical narrative a broader understanding of the importance of faith-based higher education in the American religious landscape.

- Barry H. Corey, Ph.D.
President of Biola University
Author of *Love Kindness: Discover the Power of a Forgotten Christian Virtue* and *Make the Most of It: A Guide to Loving Your College Years*

Pioneering Spirit: Chronicles of Evangel College's First 25 Years: 1955-1980" is an excellent qualitative documentation of the early years of Evangel College. Dr. Hector Cruz capitalized on the people and practices that became the deeply rooted foundation of the university. In addition, Dr. Cruz brings to life some of the victories and challenges that made the pursuit of truth and integration of faith and learning the time honored principles at the core of Evangel College then and Evangel University today.

- Dr. Jon Spence
Class of 1988, Chief Academic Officer

Dr. Cruz's research has resulted in an important, in-depth analysis of the formation of Evangel University. This resource chronicles the key steps — and a few missteps — taken during the first 25 years of Evangel's existence. He did a masterful job of researching and analyzing archived documents and oral histories, as well as his own surveys and interviews with a wide variety of people who lived, studied and worked at Evangel College during those early years.

- Mr. Paul K. Logsdon
Class of 1977, Public Relations Director 1988-2020

In this penetrating and fascinating tome, Dr. Hector Cruz presents the results of his intensive study of the leadership of Evangel College (now University). He studies the purposes of the first national university of the recently formed Assemblies of God in America (1955-1980), From Reverend Ralph Riggs to Presidents Dr. Klaude Kendrick, J. Robert Ashcroft, and Robert Spence, leadership labored to create a Pentecostal institution to rival Christian schools of recent advent.

Hector Cruz is an excellent scholar, carefully working with many strands of primary materials. He discovers many achievements. However, when he deals with occasional missteps, he treats these with great caution and wisdom. Much can be learned from a careful reading of this text.

I am delighted to endorse Cruz' work.

- Dr. Stanley M. Burgess
Evangel College Faculty 1959-1976

Today Evangel University is a very successful, thriving and forward-moving college that went through a rough start in the early 1950's. Hector did an excellent job showing how the paradigm of the Assemblies of God had to shift before embracing a vision of starting a private liberal arts college that would train young people to succeed in the secular world. After searching through archives, newspaper articles, quotes and writings of leaders from those years, he found a true picture of the struggles, sacrifices and determination many went through to bring Evangel University into existence. To make his findings complete, he interviewed and surveyed several alumni from those early years, resulting in an excellent assessment of how the college was finally established in 1955.

- Ms. Gloria Karmarkovic
Class of 1968, daughter of Dr. Alexander Kamarkovic

Dr. Hector Cruz thoroughly unpacks and explores the lived experiences of students, faculty, and administrators learning and serving on Evangel University's campus from 1955 to 1980. His book picks up where "From Opposition to Opening" by Dr. Barry Corey leaves off, providing readers insights from first-hand accounts of the dedication and loyalty involved in launching and building a strong Christian liberal arts college amid equal parts enthusiasm, skepticism, and opposition. Anyone serving in higher education will resonate with this text and appreciate Hector's narrative told through the lens of people who experienced life transformation on Evangel's campus.

- Dr. Shonna Crawford
Class of 2000, former Education Department Chair, Evangel University
Convoy of Hope, Vice President, Convoy: Women

The story of the men and women who committed themselves wholly to God's mission of raising up generations of Spirit-filled leaders in business, government, the military, education, medicine, and other non-ministerial professions in the most unlikely of settings needs to be told and celebrated. Dr. Bary Corey started the story by detailing the founding of the Evangel University until its opening in 1955. Dr. Hector Cruz took up the task of documenting the 25 years that followed the opening of the school. Two scriptures come to mind as I consider Dr. Hector Cruz's narrative of the first 25 years of Evangel University. The first verse recognizes that only God could institute and fulfil the mission of building a prestigious university on the grounds of an abandoned WWII army hospital where students were housed, and classes and chapels held in cold, drafty barracks.

1 Corinthians 1:27a (NIV) But God chose the foolish things of the world to shame the wise.

The second scripture is engraved on clock tower as a reminder those invested in the university's success who began and continues the work.

I Samuel 7:12 "Thus far the LORD has helped us."

Telling the story is important for two reasons. The first is to collect in writing the lived experiences of the early students, faculty, and school leaders before they are lost forever and synthesize their experiences with the historical events occurring between 1955 and 1980. The second, and most important, is to glorify God who set the whole unlikely adventure into motion. To date, thousands of alumni from Evangel have populated prestigious positions across the world. The historical narrative by Dr. Cruz addresses how this tiny college survived and thrived given the improbable setting for an institution of higher learning. The conclusion is the mission and institution were God-ordained and God-blessed. The barracks are long gone, but the passion built in the alumni for service to God and man has produced and continues to produce great fruit.

- Dr. Susan Langston
Professor Emeritus of Education
Director of Dissertation Research
Doctor of Education Program
Evangel University

PIONEERING SPIRIT
Chronicles of Evangel College's First 25 Years
1955-1980

HECTOR CRUZ

PIONEERING SPIRIT
Chronicles of Evangel College's First 25 Years
1955-1980

Copyright © 2024. All rights reserved. Except for brief quotations in critical publications or reviews, no part of this book may be reproduced in any manner without prior written permission from the author.

Scripture quotations marked (NIV) are taken from the Holy Bible, New International Version®, NIV®. Copyright © 1973, 1978, 1984, 2011 by Biblica, Inc.™ Used by permission of Zondervan. All rights reserved worldwide. www.zondervan.com The "NIV" and "New International Version" are trademarks registered in the United States Patent and Trademark Office by Biblica, Inc.™

Scripture quotations from The Authorized (King James) Version. Rights in the Authorized Version in the United Kingdom are vested in the Crown. Reproduced by permission of the Crown's patentee, Cambridge University Press.

All photos used with permission from Evangel University.

Cover design and interior layout design by Uberwriters, LLC.
www.uberwriters.com

ISBN: 979-8-9914196-0-4 Paperback
ISBN: 979-8-9914196-1-1 eBook

Dedication

In honor of:
My wife, Eden Cruz,

who has offered her unwavering support of this pursuit through every high and low. Her belief in me has carried me through the many times I questioned myself.

My children, Noah, David, and Selah,

whose prayers and interest in this process has been inspiring and reassuring. To hear them pray for me and ask questions has meant more to me than they will ever know.

The early leaders of Evangel,

who quite literally created something out of nothing through shrewd determination, unwavering dedication, and steely resolve that this was a mission worth risking everything to fulfill. Riggs, Kendrick, Ashcroft, Spence, and so many others from those early years changed the course of history for individuals, families, and an entire denomination because of their leadership. I can only imagine the prayers that are still being answered from those "pioneers."

I pray this work is worthy of their sacrifices.

Contents

Endorsements .... *ii*
Dedication .... *ix*
List of Figures .... *xiii*
Foreword .... *xv*
Preface .... *ixx*
Acknowledgements .... *xxi*

Chapter 1: Introduction 1
Chapter 2: Literature Review 27
Chapter 3: Research Design and Methodology 51
Chapter 4: A Historical Narrative of the
       First 25 Years of Evangel University 69
Chapter 5: Presentation of Findings 145
Chapter 6: Discussion 185

References *215*
Appendices *227*
About the Author *251*

List of Figures

1. Kendrick Presidency Enrollment Trend 81
2. Kendrick Presidency - Contributions, Enrollment Income, Total Income 83
3. The original TRUTH seal 91
4. Ashcroft Presidency Enrollment Trend 112
5. Ashcroft Presidency - Tuition Per Hour Cost Trend ... 113
6. Ashcroft Presidency - Contributions, Enrollment Income, Total Income 114
7. Spence Presidency Enrollment Trend 134
8. Spence Presidency - Tuition Per Hour Cost Trend ... 134
9. Spence Presidency - Contributions, Enrollment Income, Total Income 135
10. First 25 Years Enrollment Trend - 1955-1980 135
11. First 25 Years - Tuition Per Hour Cost 136
12. First 25 Years - Contributions, Enrollment Income, Total Income 136
13. Aerial Shot of Evangel College Campus, circa 1955 138
14. Interior of Barracks Hallway 139
15. Aerial Shot of Evangel College Campus, circa 1980 140
16. Campus Shot of Barracks 141
17. Survey Participant Gender 150
18. Home Town Size 151

19. Impact on Decision to Attend Evangel 152
20. Evangel University has been successful in perpetuating the Pentecostal tradition of the AG 152
21. Evangel has provided higher education for students who were called in areas outside of vocational church ministry 153
22. The university mission should include perpetuating the AG as a fellowship or denomination 154
23. Biggest Influence on Spiritual Growth 156
24. My Evangel experience 158
25. Actual Placard from J. Robert Ashcroft's desk 161
26. How did you first learn about Evangel? 165
27. Church Affiliation Prior to Evangel 178
28. Church Affiliation Immediately After Evangel 179
29. Church Affiliation Today (2023) 180

Foreword

I have come to the conclusion that the stories of institutions of higher education are epics, not short stories. The story of any university that has endured beyond 50 years has many chapters if not volumes. This conclusion comes having served over 45 years in a variety of roles in both public and Christian higher education. My professional journey brought me back to where my own story began more than 50 years ago as an undergraduate student at what was then Evangel College.

I am writing this as a retired university president and having recently attended Evangel University's sixty-fifth commencement where the commencement speaker was Admiral Vern Clark, retired Chief of Naval Operations, a 1967 graduate of Evangel, and a personal friend. As Admiral Clark addressed the 2024 graduates, he reflected on the enduring impact that Evangel had on him as an undergraduate student and his deep appreciation that the founding vision of Evangel to nurture both the life of the spirit and the life of the mind has endured.

The enduring vision of Evangel University, what I now identify as its deep DNA, has always been rooted in the integration of faith and learning and helping students discover their vocational calling, recognizing that vocational calling encompasses all areas of vocational service. Thus, Admiral Clark's service as Chief of Naval Operations is celebrated as a sacred calling in the same way as a graduate serving as a missionary or pastor.

Last year was my 50th class reunion, and it was a joy to reconnect with many fellow classmates and reflect again on the impact that one small Christian university had on so many lives. One of the highlights of our celebration dinner was honoring a number of faculty still living. It was important to us to let these men and women know that their investment in our lives – both in the classroom and beyond – was significant in shaping the men and women we had become and contributing to Evangel's DNA that continues to endure all these years later.

I wasn't surprised when Hector Cruz asked what I thought of his dissertation research topic and would I be willing to participate as one who graduated during Evangel's first 25 years. Hector, now Dr. Cruz, earned each of his three degrees at Evangel. I met him shortly after returning to serve as Evangel's fourth president in 2013. At the time he was serving in Financial Aid and then moved to Alumni Relations and Advancement. His ability to connect with alumni, his desire to understand their journeys, his deep love for his alma mater, and his passion for learning and using data to inform his work culminated in the research reported here.

While his study is limited to his alma mater, many of his findings are consistent with what other campus-based research, especially among Christian universities, has reported. First, leadership matters. His documented historical narrative of Evangel's first three presidents highlights what faculty and alumni have pointed to that impacted them most. These leaders each demonstrated a self-sacrificing, humble leadership and in doing so encouraged by their actions and lives the same commitment among faculty, staff, and students. Today we call this a Level 5 leader or what Jim Collins' research identifies as those executive leaders who demonstrate the paradoxical combination of genuine personal humility and professional will.

Second, relationships matter. The greatest enduring impact in the lives of graduates across the years remains the relationships they had with their faculty and fellow students. Faculty were committed to investing in their students, encouraging the deep integration of learning and faith, demonstrating through their own lives what it looks like to love God deeply with one's mind, heart, and hands extended in service. Their investment extended beyond the classroom often hosting students in their homes, joining them in chapel and the cafeteria, sitting with them at campus events, having extended office hours to be available.

The residential campus experience, especially during the early years while the campus was being transformed from a WWII army hospital to the beautiful campus of today, provided opportunities for deep friendships and shared experiences with fellow students. Student life extended far beyond the classroom where lifelong friendships persist today.

Hector's work adds to the growing body of research that reflects on what most deeply impacts students in an enduring way far beyond the awarding of a degree to having meaningful lives both in their vocational careers and in their personal lives. This may be even more vital today as we are increasingly aware of the stress, depression, and sense of isolation reported among university students, even on Christian university campuses.

It is easy to think the challenges and turbulent times today in the world and in the world of higher education in particular are somehow unique. Reviewing our history and the stories of our alumni, remembering how our institutions navigated other turbulent seasons, reflecting on what truly matters as we continue to invest in this and future generations of students, may be just what we need today to persevere and continue to produce graduates who will live as the presence of Christ in the world and in their homes. Campuses, technologies, academic disciplines all continue to evolve as does how we deliver services. What must endure is that deep DNA of our institutions which focuses on that timeless charge found in Micah 6:8 – to act justly, to love mercy, and to walk humbly with our God.

Carol Taylor, PhD
Retired Evangel University President

Preface

In the annals of higher education, the story of Evangel College (now University) serves as a compelling example of vision, perseverance, and adaptation, with a profound Pentecostal underpinning.

Within the corridors of academia, where tradition and innovation often collide, Evangel College emerged as a beacon of distinction, rooted firmly in the fertile soil of Pentecostal belief. Yet, as the first Pentecostal liberal arts institution of its kind, its genesis was met with a curious dichotomy: while the institution sought to perpetuate the faith and belief systems of the Assemblies of God denomination, it grappled with the denomination's historical ambivalence toward higher education.

As custodians of this new institution, the founding visionaries of Evangel College embarked on a journey fraught with challenges and triumphs. This historical narrative delves into the formative years of the institution, tracing its trajectory through the eyes and voices of alumni and leaders who bore witness to its evolution.

The journey chronicled in these pages, explores the institution's humble beginnings to its achievement of academic accreditation and programmatic expansion. With intriguing tales of struggle and triumph, this chronicle grapples with the nuanced interplay between institutional growth and the perpetuation of Pentecostal belief systems.

Drawing upon firsthand accounts and archival records, this narrative endeavors to explore the intricate dance between faith and academia, shedding light on the transformative power of education within a religious context. What role did faculty play in the maturation and development of those pioneering students? Was the Holy Spirit at work through the process of accreditation? Did the physical location, campus, and buildings have something to do with the resilience, vision, and enduring spirit of inquiry which were embedded from the start?

This work was born out of the author's journey through completion of his dissertation as part of the Ed.D in Educational Leadership program at Evangel University. The historical account exists mostly in Chapter 4, with Chapters 1, 2, and 3 providing research, academic, and institutional context for how the work came together. Chapters 5 and 6 detail the outcomes and results from the objective and subjective analysis which was conducted, including several relevant and applicable findings which could lead the institution into the future.

As we embark on this fascinating journey into the leading Pentecostal higher education institution, may we glean insights, inspiration, and a deeper appreciation for the symbiotic relationship between faith and learning.

Acknowledgements

Thank you to my advisor and committee chair Dr. Susan Langston. The interest you took in this research helped me to commit to seeing it through to completion. Your enthusiasm was affirming and inspirational for me. You were so gracious and patient with me through every step. Thank you to my dissertation committee Dr. Shonna Crawford, Dr. Jon Spence, and Dr. Stanley Burgess. Your time, interest, and feedback during this process pulled thoughts and ideas out of me I did not know existed. Thank you to Dr. Michael Kolstad for granting your blessing to follow this pursuit. Thank you to Dr. Jeff Fulks for your willingness to listen and provide feedback. You were the very first person I remember meeting on campus and the first who told me we were ALL called. That changed the trajectory of my life. Thank you to Dr. Barry Corey who was always quick to respond to an email and even schedule phone calls to help me hone the focus of this research and provide perspective on the incredible work he did to lay the foundation for this study. I am humbled to even attempt to build on the work you have done. Thank you to Paul Logsdon, my office "roommate" for a time for helping me identify a strong list of interview candidates. I am so grateful for your friendship and for your ability to connect anything in the world to the incredible work God is doing and has done at Evangel. Thank you to the "Pioneers," those individuals who took a chance on Evangel in the first ten years of its existence. Those of us who followed are beneficiaries of your legacy. Thank You to my mother, Deborah Cruz, who helped transcribe many of the interviews. I am also thankful for the keen editing eye of Maggie Malone who helped correct things my weary eyes had missed. Thank you to those who generously supported me with scholarships. I am eternally indebted to you.

CHAPTER ONE
INTRODUCTION

Background of the Study

Evangel University opened in 1955 as a liberal arts college designed and led by a group of leaders from a relatively young Pentecostal religious denomination (Corey, 1993). Corey's (1993) narrative begins with the 1955 opening of the college and uncovers the decision-making factors and processes that produced Evangel's unique establishment by the Assemblies of God (AG). This study aims to expand Corey's research by spanning the range of 1955 to 1980, reviewing the history and experiences during the university's first 25 years of existence. It is essential to digest Corey's narrative of the university's initial history to understand the context within which it began operations. Corey lays a foundation for understanding the genesis of Evangel and provides a historical retrospective on education within the Assemblies of God denomination, the social and cultural constructs that existed during the founding years, and decisions that were specific to Evangel. The purpose of this current study is to continue the exploration of Evangel's history by building on the strong foundation of his work.

Evangel University started in barracks that remained from the World War II era and were formerly part of the O'Reilly General Hospital in Springfield, Missouri. Evangel was the first and only liberal arts postsecondary institution for a growing Pentecostal Assemblies of God denomination. The focus of the AG denomination was world evangelism and the imminent return of Jesus Christ. For some, the idea of a four-year liberal arts institution seemed counter-intuitive to the denomination's doctrine. The prevailing notion of the denominational leadership and its members was that Jesus Christ was returning soon and there was no time to educate students in business, education, humanities, or the sciences. According to some AG leaders, starting a liberal arts college seemed to take the focus off the denomination's need to evangelize and lessen the urgency to win souls for Christ. However, a few brave leaders within the AG believed a need existed within the Pentecostal faith tradition for a biblically-based liberal arts institution to train students to minister through a variety of vocations. From this belief, Evangel College was born (Corey, 1993).

The topic of higher education can be polarizing among different segments of society in many ways. This is especially true for private, Christian higher education (Frey, 2013; Hess, 2018; Horn, 2018; Lederman, 2017; Woodhouse, 2015). The national discourse around issues of funding, ideological indoctrination, and return on investment is intensifying. At the same time, a window is opening for the distinctive perspective of Christian higher education to shine through like never before (Schreiner, 2018). Increased interest and research are currently trending within Christian higher education concerning the integration of faith and learning also identified as faith-informed learning (Crider & Crider, 2020). An analysis of how Evangel alumni experienced faith integration as students and their impact and influence in the world could shed light on specific practices that effectively connect individual spiritual development with widespread community impact (Kaak, 2016).

It is fascinating to consider how a liberal arts institution was established as the flagship university for a denomination historically apathetic towards higher education (Corey, 2005). Corey's (1993) study documented decisions and actions taken to establish and begin Evangel College in 1955. During the first 25 years, the university made significant strides for a new higher education institution by gaining full accreditation within the first 10 years, building new permanent buildings on campus, and even starting a football team. Now that the university is nearing its 70th year in existence, a new study is needed to capture the history and explore the impact made in those early years. Despite growth and change on Evangel's campus and worldwide as one century gave way to another, the foundational ethos of the university remained unchanged. Those first alumni who were just embarking on their careers during the first 25 years are now able to reflect upon their full lives and many years of professional service. Exploring how the first group of students was impacted by intentionally receiving a foundation for faith integration in professional calling can illuminate the methods and practices that can ensure the long-term commitment and fulfillment of the university's mission.

Theoretical and Conceptual Frameworks
Within the context of this historical narrative, the interviews

and historical materials researched built upon the understanding of the theoretical and conceptual framework of the study. Grounded theory as described by Creswell (2014) served as the main theoretical framework of the study. Bandura's (1977) social learning theory, Vygotsky's constructivist learning theory as described by Liu and Matthews (2005), and the Christian philosophy of education described by Horton (2017) also contributed to the development of this study as theoretical and conceptual frameworks.

For Evangel, this could mean a clear direction that is illuminated particularly for Evangel based on the specific experiences of alumni who are interviewed. The real-world experiences that are collected may produce information that can lead to a new understanding of the Evangel ethos and successful mission fulfillment. There are several other theoretical and conceptual frameworks that will contribute to the lenses through which this study is conducted and viewed.

Social Learning Theory

In any educational setting, individual learning occurs as cognitive skills are developed on a social level when groups practice together and observe each other. Bandura (1971) established the Social Learning Theory (SLT) by which "in the social learning system, new patterns of behavior can be acquired through direct experience or by observing the behavior of others" (p. 3). Observational learning experience is a major contributor to a college student's success. This is especially true on a college campus where students have a similar faith background and a shared desire for spiritual and academic growth. Thus, intentionally identifying an appropriate model on campus through faculty and staff is essential to achieving the school's mission. According to Sparks (2019):

> A Review of Educational Research analysis of 46 studies found that strong teacher-student relationships were associated in both the short- and long-term with improvements on practically every measure schools care about: higher student academic engagement, attendance, grades, fewer disruptive behaviors and suspensions, and lower school dropout rates (para. 7).

Additionally, encouraging less experienced students to model behavior deemed successful by more experienced students is another component that contributes to this type of learning on campus.

Bandura (1971) explained how, through appropriate modeling, future consequences can be converted into current motivators that influence behavior in a similar way to actual consequences. In the Evangel context, these "future consequences" were modeled by the faculty who were employed and served as the motivators for current students and influenced their behavior. The author also determined individuals must understand what is being reinforced within their learning environment for successful learning to occur (Bandura, 1971). Bandura (1971) contended:

> According to social learning theory, behavior is learned, at least in rough form, before it is performed. By observing a model of the desired behavior, an individual forms an idea of how response components must be combined and temporally sequenced to produce new behavioral configurations (p. 8).

Corey (1993) found in the early years there was great emphasis on identifying and employing faculty and staff members who would model desired behavior for students to emulate while attending Evangel. Therefore, the residential component of life at Evangel and the atmosphere it created was integral to the early success of the students. Ultimately, the importance the early founders placed on identifying exemplary models for students in the new institution is strongly supported by Bandura's (1971) social learning theory.

Bandura (1971) proffered that much social learning occurs based on casual or studied observation of exemplary models and added, "It is frequently difficult to convey through words the same amount of information contained in pictorial or live demonstrations" (p. 10). When multiple professors model desired behaviors, students are provided with the option to select one or more models as their primary example(s) of behavior. This is consistent with Bandura's (1971) contention that "observers may select one or more of the models as the primary source of behavior, but they rarely restrict their imitation to a single source, nor do they adopt all of the characteristics of the preferred model" (p. 11). In the early days at Evangel, and yet still today, this is significant since professors did more than just teach. They also advised in scheduling, mentored, and sat alongside students in chapel services, on-campus events, and activities. The modeling they practiced was not relegated to the classroom.

Constructivist Learning Theory

Constructivist Learning Theory (CLT) is the second theory that supports this study. Piaget was one of the first theorists to promote constructivism, and Vygotsky perpetuated the theory through his focus on social learning. In Piaget's theory of cognitive development, a child's learning was due to the progressive reorganization of mental processes and thinking that resulted from natural biological maturation and environmental experiences (Mcleod, 2018). The adaptation processes described in Piaget's theory are key to the research in this study, specifically, the focus on how learning is adapted to enable the transition from stages of equilibrium to assimilation to accommodation (Mcleod, 2018). "Equilibrium occurs when a child's schemas can deal with most new information through assimilation" (Mclcod, 2018, Equilibrium scction). A schema, according to Piaget is "a cohesive, repeatable action sequence possessing component actions that are tightly interconnected and governed by core meaning" (as cited in Mcleod, 2018, Schemas section). Adapting one's schemas as new information is learned and experienced is the key to intellectual growth. According to Piaget's theory, equilibrium is the driving force throughout the learning process as the cognitive dissonance addressed by inquiring minds learning and experiencing new information must be assimilated into pre-existing learning schemas or accommodated by adjusting existing schemas to include the new information (Mcleod, 2018).

Liu and Matthews (2005) explained by the 1980s and 1990s constructivism emerged as the leading metaphor or theory on human learning. The authors noted that in the 20th century, "The fact that constructivists, of whatever ilk, consensually hold that knowledge is not mechanically acquired, but actively constructed within the constraints and offerings of the learning environment, was commonly regarded as a shift in paradigm in educational psychology" (Liu & Matthews, 2005, p. 387). The social context and environment for a learner along with the role of social collectivity was of central importance to Vygotsky's constructivist philosophy. Liu and Matthews (2005) pointed out that, according to Vygotsky, "Learners are believed to be encultured into their learning community and appropriate knowledge, based on their existent understanding, through their interaction with the immediate learning environment" (p. 388).

It is important to have an accurate understanding of Vygotsky's view on paradigms to understand his perspective on education and learning. "Paradigms are comparable to intentional truth and a *priori* knowledge, which cannot be objectively or empirically asserted, only individually represented and internally experienced" (Liu & Matthews, 2005, p. 390). The communal and collective nature of the residential experience on campus in the early years of Evangel created an environment ripe for the type of education Vygotsky espoused. "In this sense, perhaps for Vygotsky the central aim of education is not so much to develop consciousness, but to develop the all-rounded personality and freedom of consciousness from social divisions" (Liu & Matthews, 2005, p. 396). The experience, as reported by many alumni experiences, was all-encompassing. Students from many different backgrounds were united in a desire to grow in their faith and discover their calling and career. They may have entered Evangel with a certain set of paradigms, and left having shifted their paradigms based on their academic preparation and deepened faith understanding.

Christian Philosophy of Education

Since Evangel's curriculum and ethos were founded on Christian principles, the Christian Philosophy of Education developed by Horton provides an additional conceptual framework for this study. Horton (2017) described biblical Christianity as "a system of certain basic truths that God has revealed" (p. 4). The basic tenets of the Christian faith are shared across many other denominations, both Pentecostal and non-Pentecostal. These include the following beliefs:

- God created man in his own image (Gen. 1:26-27).
- The image of God in man was marred when man fell through disobedience to his Creator (Gen 3).
- God has provided for the restoration of His image in man through the person and work of Jesus Christ (2 Cor. 5:17)
- Salvation is achieved through placing one's faith and belief in Jesus Christ (John 3:16)

These are the elements of the Christian faith that directly impact an individual's salvation. Through accepting salvation, achieved when Jesus Christ died for the sin of humanity, and believing that Jesus Christ is Lord of all, the individual's sins are forgiven, righteousness before God is achieved, and the individual secures an eternal place in Heaven (John 3:16). Many denominations include other belief systems and frameworks that add specificity to their strand of faith. For example, the AG established its statement of 16 fundamental truths that are central to the fundamental beliefs and guiding principles of the denomination. From the official statement on these fundamental truths, "No claim is made that it covers all Biblical truth, only that it covers our need as to these fundamental doctrines" (Assemblies of God 16 Fundamental Truths, 2022, para. 1). It is important to understand the general nature of the Christian Philosophy of Education addressed in this section along with the more specific belief system and structure of the AG to broaden the understanding of the unique context and mission of Evangel University. Horton (2017) explained, "The purpose of Christian education is the directing of the process of human development toward God's objective for man: godliness of character and action" (p. 6).

Careful examination of Corey's (1993) work reveals how central the Christian Philosophy of Education was to the development of Evangel. As a denomination closely linked to the holiness tradition, the focus on developing young people in godliness of character was of central concern. As Corey (1993) indicates, "Pure Christianity, according to those of the late nineteenth-century holiness followings, could never harmonize with the culture man created" (p. 7). How a person appeared and the places one frequented were visual indicators of a person's relationship with Jesus Christ according to early Holiness tradition.

Additionally, the focus on the imminent return of Christ spurred Evangel founders to incorporate an emphasis on faith in action that resulted in international mission service projects. With the foundational belief that all people are fallen and in need of salvation, as described in this conceptual framework, early university leaders believed students needed service experiences in missions regardless of whether their future careers were related to vocational ministry. The idea that ministry for Christ was an integral component of success in all vocations created a unique sense of calling for students preparing for a variety of careers.

An important element of successful Christian education directly relates to the salvation experience and willingness of the learners to deepen their faith. In the AG context, it is important to bring students to faith in Christ and perpetuate the AG tradition. Horton (2017) indicated a regenerated (or salvation) experience and willingness on behalf of the student are prerequisites for Christian education to successfully carry out its purpose. "Christian education proper begins with spiritual rebirth, when the life of God is communicated to the soul" (Horton, 2017, p. 6). Included in this philosophy is a missional element within the school to reach students who have not yet committed to Christ and lead them to a salvation experience. As Horton (2017) explained, "To make children and even unregenerated adults 'wise unto salvation' is no less a legitimate function of Christian education today" (p. 7).

As a conceptual framework, the philosophy of Christian education stems from the sole foundation that all truth is God's truth. This understanding is often repeated within Christian education as a mantra and reminder that the Bible must be the sole source of understanding. Horton (2017) expressed this philosophical foundation by detailing:

> The whole body of Christian educational theory rests on the recognition that all truth is of God. He is the God of truth (Ps 31:5); His Son is the Lord of truth (Jn 14:6); His Spirit is the Spirit of truth (Jn 14:16-17). All truth, whether discerned or undiscerned by man, springs from

a single source and therefore consists as one harmonious whole. Consequently, God's written self-revelation is the starting point of all rational inquiry and the guide to all interpretation of reality. (p. 9).

Proper biblical training and training in the liberal arts are not mutually exclusive emphases. Rather, according to Horton (2017), they are complementary of each other. The author explained:

> Especially is God revealed in His rational creation, man, who having been created in the image of God is the highest of God's works on earth. It is for this reason that the Christian school gives emphasis to the humanities: the study of man's language, his literature, his artistic achievements, the record of his history, the logic of his mathematical reasoning, and the other forms of his personal and cultural expression. (Horton, 2017, p. 11)

For Evangel, this underpins the often quoted phrase that all truth is God's truth no matter where it is found. The significance of the faith journey does not remain confined within the walls of the church, but the belief that God is found in every aspect of life.

Finally, a proper understanding of the Christian philosophy of education has elements that directly relate to Bandura's social learning theory and Piaget's and Vygotsky's constructivist approaches. Students in Christian education, often learn through modeling from the Christian teachers leading them in their coursework and career development. This type of teacher-student relationship building was another core emphasis in the early years of Evangel and will continue to be so if its mission is to prevail. The emphasis on modeling by teachers is supported by Horton (2017) who maintained, "It is for this reason that the Christian school must pay careful attention to the character and conduct of its teachers. No school that is careless concerning the Christlikeness of its teachers can be sure to fulfill the purpose of Christian education" (Horton, 2017, p. 14).

Statement of the Problem

Corey's (1993) research on the decision-making structures that led to the formation of Evangel University filled a need to understand the ethos of a wholly committed Christian institution of higher education. Since his work, the history of the school has been collected and archived, but a historical narrative of Evangel since its inception in 1955 does not currently exist. The different pieces of this important history exist, but in component and disconnected pieces. They remain as pieces of data in need of compilation into useful information.

Evangel is still considered young within the context of higher education, yet examination of its relatively short history reveals a growing legacy through the world-changing actions and influence of its alumni. Former professors, alumni, and administrators who were present at the founding and are still alive can contribute firsthand accounts of the history of the university. Their accounts are essential to produce an accurate portrayal and understanding of the early years of a denominational institution and how it persisted. Lived experiences that are recorded and shared can have meaningful impact on a university in perpetuity. These experiences, accurately recorded and shared, can provide depth of insight into the core mission and context of the university. By accurately analyzing these formative years of the university, truths can be gleaned that will ensure the mission of the University continues to drive decision-making of the future.

The AG has a complex history related to higher education, and the idea of a liberal arts institution within the AG was approached with apprehension and uncertainty (Yong, 2021). Evangel is the only institution within the denomination founded with a mission for liberal arts education. Every other AG institution was founded as a Bible school focused on ministerial training and has added liberal arts elements over time. While seemingly small, the difference in focus among the universities presents an opportunity to explore how the liberal arts focus shaped the first 25 years of the institution. To address the problem of a missing comprehensive historical narrative of the university effectively, the focus of this historical narrative will cover the first 25 years of operation for the institution in the years 1955 to 1980. This will allow for a more focused and deeper analysis of the important events that occurred during that era as opposed to researching the entire history to the point of this writing. In addition to the internal issues and missing pieces this study seeks to address, there is a growing body of external analysis that has alarming implications for higher education.

In recent years, an increasing number of educational experts have made bold claims regarding higher education (Frey, 2013; Hess, 2018; Horn, 2018; Lederman, 2017; Woodhouse, 2015). Many of these claims will most negatively impact small, private institutions like Evangel. Frey (2013) predicted, "We will begin to see the mass failure of traditional colleges. But out of this will come an entire new education era unlike anything we have ever seen" (para. 8). Woodhouse (2015) agreed, "Closure rates of small colleges and universities will triple in the coming years, and mergers will double" (para. 1). In 2017, Clayton Christensen, considered to be the father of the theory of disruption innovation, shared his belief that half of all colleges would close within a decade and stated it may even be less time than that based on the growth of online education (as cited in Lederman, 2017). This claim was further substantiated by mass media outlets including CNBC and Forbes (Hess, 2018; Horn, 2018).

However, there does seem to be hope for institutions such as Evangel that focus on the relationship between faculty and students. As Hess (2018) noted:

> Fortunately, Christensen says that there is one thing that online education will not be able to replace. In his research, he found that most of the successful alumni who gave generous donations to their alma maters did so because a specific professor or coach inspired them. (para. 7)

The implication that personal relationships matter to student success supports the importance of in-person residential experiences. It also helps to explain why, even in difficult economic seasons, students continue to choose a small, private college dedicated to facilitating relationships over larger, less expensive options.

The recent COVID-19 pandemic initiated a pivotal season of economic and social change for institutions of higher education. Prior to COVID-19, institutions were struggling with decreasing student enrollment due to fewer college-age students, the economic impact caused by the Great Recession of the early 2000s, and the growth of online learning options

(Falk et al., 2020). The economic and social shutdown response to the pandemic increased fears that traditional colleges and universities are becoming obsolete and will not survive. Falk et al. (2020) advised, "Education is likely to dramatically change; we are not going back to the old normal, and colleges must respond" (para. 51). The authors agreed with Frey's (2013) prediction that traditional colleges would continue to fail and indicated the pandemic was revealing the growing vulnerabilities within small higher education institutions (Falk et al., 2020). More recently, Lederman (2021) revealed, "More public and private two-year and four-year colleges closed or merged between 2019-20 and 2020-21 than was true for for-profit institutions, a change from recent trends" (para. 1).

Purpose of the Study

The purpose of this study is to explore by synthesizing common themes derived from firsthand accounts of Evangel alumni, former professors, and administrators who lived the history during the period being studied into a historical narrative. The work builds on Corey's (1993) dissertation and Corey's (2005) historical narrative detailing the founding of the institution. An additional purpose of the collective narrative is to identify events, experiences, and strategies that contributed to the institutional persistence, academic preparation, and flourishing faith integration that characterized the Evangel University experience since its founding in 1955.

To narrow the focus of the study, the narrative only includes perspectives from the first 25 years (1955 – 1980) of Evangel's history. An equally important purpose of this study is to discover how the original mission of the institution was executed at

Evangel within the first 25 years. This discovery will help university leaders establish vision for the future while continuing to work toward mission fulfillment. Additionally, this study will carry forward the historical narrative established through Corey's work while establishing a precedent on how to conduct future studies on the university in quarter-century increments. As the university ages, a growing body of historical narratives and methodologies will contribute to consistent understanding of how the mission is being understood and executed on campus and in the lives of alumni.

Significance of the Study

As Winston Churchill stated, "Those who do not learn from history are doomed to repeat it." (Geller, 2018, para. 39) Within the context of a higher education institution focused on continuous improvement, growth, and development, repeating the past is not the goal. However, compiling the oral histories and anecdotal elements of past successes into a well-developed historical narrative can help leaders at Christian universities such as Evangel University move confidently into the future with a firm understanding of best practices.

Findings of this study will contribute to the academic literature regarding leadership in Christian higher education. Results will also make a significant contribution to the future of Evangel over the course of the next several decades. The findings of this study will help university leaders increase the intentionality with which students are encouraged and empowered to engage in Spirit-filled learning experiences. This is a distinctive of the Pentecostal foundation of the university where the integration of faith and learning coincides with the active work of the Holy

Spirit. The collective narrative will also preserve and present the history of the first quarter-century of the university's existence through the recorded firsthand accounts of participants. Findings of the study will also allow for an increased understanding of how to perpetuate a Pentecostal heritage, foundational beliefs, and worldview within the Christian higher education framework.

By understanding the historical context along with the qualitative experience of alumni, university leaders can more effectively position the University to meet the demands of the next generation of students while becoming a leading institution within the Christian higher education community. Finally, this study may serve as a blueprint for other universities lacking a historical narrative to conduct their own study in establishing how their institutions may be able to prevail in the field of Christian higher education.

Research Questions

The first 25 years of operational existence of Evangel University, a private Christian university in the midwestern United States, are analyzed in this study. This historical analysis and qualitative phenomenological study are meant to provide foundational context for how the university established its founding ethos from pre-existing theory (before 1955) to tangible mission execution (1955 - 1980). Creswell (2014) explains the central question as a broad question that asks for an exploration of the central phenomenon of concept in a study. As such, the following central question guided this study:

> What practices from the first twenty-five years of Evangel University can be applied to positive, successful mission fulfillment in the future?

The following sub-questions support the study's inquiry:

1. How do alumni perceive the spiritual development they experienced while at Evangel University impacted their personal and professional lives?
2. What experiences do alumni, faculty, and staff from the first 25 years share from their time at Evangel?
3. What historical events during the first 25 years of Evangel University's existence shaped the foundational ethos of the institution?
4. What key insights do alumni share across their respective careers and contexts?

Limitations and Assumptions

In this qualitative phenomenological study, a discussion of the limitations and assumptions is key to understanding how external factors and internal beliefs may influence inferences and interpretations drawn from the study. Limitations to a study can also be considered constraints. They include any element of the study, research, or researcher's context that inhibit the study in any way. Assumptions can be considered biases that may impact the collection of the data or the interpretation of the data after it is collected. A deeper analysis of the limitations and assumptions as they relate to this study follows.

Limitations

There are several limitations to this study. First, this is a historical analysis of a single university within the private, Christian higher education context in the midwestern United States. The unique history of Evangel University does not match the history of other institutions, even those within the same denomination.

As such, this research may not be replicable, nor the findings of this study be applicable to other institutions.

Second, Evangel maintains a comprehensive database of alumni contact information that is only as accurate as the updates provided by alumni. For the survey component of the study, there are 6,278 alumni who attended within the timeframe being researched (1955-1980). Of that number of alumni, 5,609 are still living, and only 2,594 email addresses (46%) are available, some of which may not be updated or open to receiving emails from the Evangel alumni office. Furthermore, of the alumni who receive the emailed survey, not all will respond. Responses will be collected from those who are willing to respond. This will inhibit the amount of data to be collected by mass survey.

Third, while some faculty, students, and administrators were available to conduct personal interviews, many key contributors from this timeframe were unavailable or have passed away. Sadly, the personal experiences of these individuals cannot be included in this study's data.

Fourth, the bias of the researcher must be included as a limitation. The researcher is an undergraduate and graduate alumnus of the institution being studied. The researcher also works for the institution in a fulltime staff capacity, as an adjunct faculty member, and is taking courses through a doctoral program at the institution. While steps were taken to mitigate bias in data collection, the researcher's association with the university may impact the interpretation of data and inferences drawn from the study's results.

Assumptions

There are several assumptions that guided the development of this study. These assumptions are related to the stories shared by Evangel alumni of their experiences as students, the personal experiences of the researcher who is a current student and alumnus of the university, and current research in the field.

The first assumption is that the current emphases on the integration of faith and learning and discovery of vocational calling have always existed as part of the experience at the university. Personal interviews and mass surveys will confirm or deny this assumption through the analysis of the research results.

The second assumption relates to the idea that all institutions of higher education of any kind will acknowledge they too practice instilling academic excellence within their students through their faculty. Faith integration and spiritual development are distinctives for Evangel University compared to public and non-Christian institutions, but other Christian institutions would most likely claim these distinctives as well (Hammond, 2019). Consequently, the need is accentuated for university leadership to identify how the distinctives are contextually actualized to ensure future success of mission fulfilment.

A third assumption is most alumni from the timeframe being researched will have a desire to participate in the study being that most have reached a reflective stage in their careers. This assumption will be tested when the mass survey is sent and responses are collected.

A fourth assumption is based on the current research in the field related to Christian higher education. Examples of this include how Davis (2018) indicates a challenge in defining faith integration and spiritual formation amongst AG higher education institutions. Corey (1993) tells the story of the founding of Evangel and may be contradicted by lived experiences of individual alumni. Strahan (1955) compiled the introductory curriculum for Evangel as his dissertation research. His findings may also be contradicted by the lived experiences of the students at the time. Updated research gleaned by this study will support or deny some of these assumptions.

Definition of Key Terms

To provide appropriate context and understanding for this study, several terms must be properly defined. Davis (2018) attempted to define the terms Faith Integration and Spiritual Development, but was unable to define either term in a meaningful or widely accepted fashion. A definition for each of these terms, and others, is presented here for the context of this study.

Evangel University

Evangel University (EU), or Evangel College (EC) as it was known during the time period of this study, is a private, Christian liberal arts university in Springfield, Missouri. Their mission is to educate and equip students to become Spirit-empowered servants of God who impact the Church and society globally.

Alumni, Faculty, Staff, and Administrators

This group formed the group of individuals who contributed to the successful founding of the university. This group consisted of current students between 1955 and 1980 who are now alumni and employees who were professors, staff members, and leaders during the same time period.

Denomination

A denomination, in this context, is considered a particular sect or specific stream of Christianity that adheres to a distinctive set of beliefs or understandings.

Holiness

In this study, the term holiness refers to the holiness movement which was a branch of John Wesley's Methodism. The holiness movement was intent on reasserting and extending the pietistic values within the church and the larger culture (Corey, 1993)

Assemblies of God

The Assemblies of God was founded in 1914 in Hot Springs, Arkansas with 300 people at the founding convention. Today there are nearly 13,000 churches in the U.S. with over 3 million members and adherents. There are more than 69 million Assemblies of God members worldwide, making the Assemblies of God the world's largest Pentecostal denomination (About the AG, n.d.).

Pentecostal

Merriam-Webster dictionary defines Pentecostal as relating to, or constituting any of various Christian religious bodies that emphasize individual experiences of grace, spiritual gifts (such as glossolalia and faith healing), expressive worship, and evangelism.

Integration of Faith and Learning

This phrase has been widely used and adopted within the Evangel context. The intention and connotation is that an individual's faith should be fully integrated within the context of their education regardless of the subject matter. For example, a person's faith should inform how they understand whichever subject they are learning. Faith is not relegated to classes on biblical history or literacy.

Spirit-Filled Learning
This term is closely connected to the idea espoused by the integration of faith and learning while incorporating the person and work of the Holy Spirit that is integral to the Pentecostal experience and belief system.

Spiritual Development
In this context, spiritual development is intended to mean the growth and maturation related to faith an individual will experience.

Evangel Pioneers
Evangel Pioneers refer to alumni who attended the University during the first ten years of existence (1955 – 1965).

Calling
Calling is another word used frequently in the Evangel context. It connotes the idea that all individuals have a unique mission in life resulting from a combination of their individual interests, innate abilities, and God's purpose.

Summary
Exploring and analyzing the initial history of Evangel will result in understanding the key distinctives that have shaped the University and the students it has produced. This improved understanding can help lead the University into the future of more intentionally educating and equipping students to become Spirit-empowered servants of God who impact the Church and society globally.

Bandura's (1977) Social Learning Theory and Vygotsky's Constructivist Framework both contribute to understanding the context on campus in its formative years. The Christian

Philosophy of Education is another cornerstone to the structure and focus of education on campus in the early years.

Without a summary of the historical record since its founding in 1955, there is a significant risk in losing important details and history that have contributed to the university's success. The impending steady decline in the number of higher education institutions, particularly small, private institutions, in the coming years highlights the importance for establishing a summary of Evangel's historical narrative. Without an accurate portrayal and understanding of the institution's history, it will be a significant challenge to continue to progress effectively as an institution long into the future.

The purpose of this research is to lay the foundation for an accurate historical narrative of the first 25 years of the university's existence. Corey's (1993) work is the building block for this effort that seeks to build on the foundation that was laid through his research. Additionally, the significance of this study is its contributions to a glaring deficiency in the summary of the historical account for the time period being researched. Furthermore, other like-minded institutions who have not established a summary historical narrative may be able to use this research as a blueprint to conduct their own study in establishing how their institutions may be able to prevail in the field of Christian higher education.

Limitations and assumptions were established to provide for transparency in the challenges related to this study and the researcher's proximity to the data and context. Through this research and the interpretation of the collected data, limitations, and assumptions will be overcome or confirmed as accurate.

An inability to collect histories from all alumni from the timeframe under study as well as the researcher's own biases are acknowledged but will be difficult to overcome.

Chapter Two provides a review of the existing literature related to the focus of this study. As a historical narrative of a particular institution, the related research covers the broad issues related to Christian higher education. Materials more specific to the institution being studied will also be presented.

CHAPTER TWO
LITERATURE REVIEW

Introduction

A review of the literature for this study will include elements related to the internal, historical narrative of the university and experiences of alumni along with external issues affecting the university in the broader context of Christian higher education. Alignment exists between the current academic literature in the field of Christian higher education and some of the experiences and narratives of alumni and leaders at the university. While the experiences of individuals at Evangel reveal common themes within the broader literature, the specific details are unique to Evangel. Subsequently, this review of the literature will attempt to combine thematic elements relevant to the broader context of higher education and specific to Evangel University.

Review of Background

Corey (1993) illuminates important factors of the decision-making process related to the founding of Evangel College. His study serves as a historical account directly revealing the "how" and indirectly the "why" of the decision making (Corey, 1993). Over the 68 years since the school's founding, much has changed both internally at Evangel and externally in society. To effectively understand the context of the institution in the first 25 years, a thorough review is needed of the decision-making processes that contributed to its success during that timeframe.

Regarding the literature, the emphasis on Christian higher education as a standalone section of research is relatively new, and certainly is considered new since the time period being studied. However, this new section of research is still helpful in understanding the context of administrator concerns and alumni experiences from the early history of Evangel.

Cascading distinctive characteristics of Evangel University are revealed in the literature. These distinctive characteristics begin with the foundation of a private Christian university in the context of the entire higher education landscape. They continue with the Pentecostal heritage of a university within the Christian higher education subset, and they end with the unique, lived experiences of alumni and leaders. A more detailed description of the themes and subthemes follows.

Introduction of Themes

Themes have been identified from a combined review of the existing literature and the oral histories of alumni. The first theme illuminates a focus on faith integration and spiritual development in education. Faith integration and spiritual development are important components of student experiences in Christian higher education. Distinctively in the Evangel context, the vernacular used to describe this theme is the integration of faith and learning. Subthemes include a historical background of faith integration and spiritual development in education within the Assemblies of God and within the curriculum at Evangel. A broader analysis of faith integration and spiritual development in Christian higher education is a second subtheme.

The second theme discusses more denominational details regarding identity and distinctive characteristics of the Assemblies of God denomination. Within this theme, the subthemes of Christian education, Evangelicalism, and Pentecostalism are reviewed and discussed. The third theme increases the focus on the personal experience of alumni at Evangel during the timeframe being studied. It is important to consider how the personal experience of alumni compares to current research explored in the previous themes of the literature. Subthemes in this section attempt to draw connections between the personal experiences and the literature reviewed.

Faith Integration and Spiritual Development in Education

Faith integration is a key distinctive of Christian higher education. However, learning from the history of the Evangel experience will highlight how the integration of faith and learning was planned and executed in the early years of the institution. This historical analysis will begin with the plans put in place by the early school leaders of the day.

Spiritual development is the natural byproduct of effective faith integration and is considered as another key distinctive of Christian higher education. Surveys of Evangel alumni will highlight the longstanding impact of their spiritual development while on campus as students.

Historical Background

There is a poignant quote in the preface of Corey's (1993) work taken from the accreditation team who made the decision to approve full accreditation of Evangel in 1965, just ten years after its founding, and it is worth repeating here:

> In its relationship to the denomination, [Evangel College] may be walking a kind of tightrope. On the one hand, the College will probably serve as a major source of change in the denomination, providing leadership as the church itself becomes more middle class and values education more highly. On the other hand, it is seen by many of its supporters as a conserver of existing attitudes and institutions, and in some ways it undoubtedly does perform that function. (Corey, 1993, p ii)

Corey (1993) contends his research affirms the latter claim in the report about the school conserving the existing attitudes, which mostly dealt with the importance of evangelism, proper spiritual development, and the person and work of the Holy Spirit, the third person in the Trinity of the Christian faith.

The topic of education was presented as a focus for the Assemblies of God even before the founding meeting in 1914. According to a 1913 publication announcing the inaugural meeting in Hot Springs, Arkansas in 1914, five reasons were given to explain the need for the meeting to unite a growing body of Pentecostals. The fifth reason listed in the announcement discussed education and the need for Pentecostal believers to develop a bible training school that included a literary department for Pentecostal young people (Corey, 1993). Over the next three decades, much debate ensued as to exactly what was meant by the term "literary department." Several different Bible training schools, Bible institutes, and even junior colleges opened and closed during that time with little development towards education outside of training ministers, missionaries, and evangelists. The prevailing notion of AG leaders and members was that the imminent return of Jesus Christ precluded any necessity for training outside of ministerial preparation.

As time went on and the denomination grew, leaders edited their perspectives that since Jesus had not yet returned, the mission to biblically train young people for jobs beyond ministry held merit. As the second generation of Assemblies of God adherents rose to prominence so did the discussion on the need for training outside of traditional vocational ministry positions. However, Corey illuminates the feelings of many Pentecostals of the day when he states they, "shuddered when they considered the denomination's investing in an institution to prepare bankers, teachers, and journalists" (Corey, 1993, p. 46). It is evident the tightrope the accrediting committee referenced in their 1965 report existed back before the university was ever in existence. The church held a common fear that they were following the same liberal path towards institutionalization that other Protestant denominations had traveled. In their view, those wayward denominations had been accelerated down that path by the increasing secularization of their church-created institutions of higher education that resulted in the colleges being unwittingly at odds with their founding visions (Corey, 1993). On the other hand, many within the Assemblies of God denomination were dually concerned with retaining the faith of the church's youth as the second generation of adherents continued to grow. What if the imminent return of Jesus Christ was not so imminent and the young people of the time went out into the world without a proper training in the Pentecostal faith tradition? Those who held this concern endeavored to utilize higher education as the primary means by which to equip young people to retain their Pentecostal heritage and faith (Corey, 1993). For this group, the answer was to provide a denominational college that could appropriately prepare young people for careers "in an environment which was not threatening to their faith" (Corey, 1993, p. 46). "Together they embarked on one of the most intense and long-lived debates in the history of the Assemblies of God movement" (Corey, 1993, p.46). This debate continues to this day.

At the 1943 convening of leaders and pastors within the Assemblies of God, known as General Council, Ralph M. Riggs was elected as the Assistant General Superintendent. In this role, he became the predominant voice in support for educational reform, and particularly for the development of a liberal arts institution to serve the denomination's youth. It was his steely resolve and tireless work that paved the way for the establishment of Evangel College. He employed the energies of several other denominational leaders, but it was Riggs who led the way.

Corey (1993) thoroughly details the decision-making process that was utilized to found Evangel College. Throughout that process, Riggs trumpeted the need for an Assemblies of God liberal arts institution. In his view, the youth within the Assemblies of God were attending institutions that were modernistic and anti-Pentecostal because they had no liberal arts options within the denomination. As such, many different statistics were shared over the years to show the number of young people walking away from the Assemblies of God denomination because of this issue. On the other side of the thin tightrope were leaders like W.I. Evans, the principal of Central Bible Institute (CBI, later Central Bible College, or CBC). In an early meeting convened by Riggs, he expressed apprehension and deep concern with regard to transitioning existing Bible schools to four-year colleges and fear of different accrediting agencies who may require degreed faculty members (Corey, 1993). Throughout his career, it seemed, Ralph Riggs walked along this tightrope within the denomination.

Because of Riggs consistency of communication and fervent promotion for a church-sponsored liberal arts college, he was known as the self-appointed activist of the idea. Riggs developed twelve arguments to express the importance and necessity for such a college (Corey, 1993, pp. 58-59):

1. Our young people deserve mental and physical development for its own sake.
2. They should be given that measure and kind of development and education which they need to meet present-day life and competition.
3. They need to have counteracted by scholarly and godly professors that measure of evolution and unbelief which has been planted in their minds in their grammar and high school days.
4. They should be protected in their higher education from the atheism, sin, and pride of our modern universities.
5. They should be aided in the proper evaluation of Christianity over against all modern ideologies.
6. They should be shown the power and wisdom of God in all the arts and sciences, for they are truly his handmaidens.
7. Our church is far behind her sister churches in this regard.

8. We and we only are responsible for our own young people.
9. Our church is crippling itself by losing so many of our best young people, our future leaders, in allowing them to be educated in other colleges.
10. The missionary fields are increasingly demanding college-trained personnel.
11. We must make our contribution toward purifying and strengthening American life.
12. More room will be provided in our Bible Institutes by the transfer to our college of any of their youngest students who are as yet too immature for theological training and who may not even be called to preach.

It can be inferred that if the imminent return of Jesus was not as imminent as once perceived, then the focus of those concerned about a liberal arts college would be placed on the adamant emphasis that the reliance and experience of the Holy Spirit be infused into the establishment and curriculum of the liberal arts institution. This was an area where Riggs and those concerned agreed.

In the very first college planning committee Riggs convened on December 28-29, 1944, eleven years before Evangel College would officially open its doors, the committee adopted Riggs' twelve needs for the college verbatim. The committee also established Pentecostal standards, or what they called safeguards, to protect the college from corruption, sin, and worldly influences. Examples of these safeguards included a requirement that all who administrate the college be baptized in the Holy Spirit with the physical evidence of speaking in

Literature Review

tongues. Students were also to maintain Pentecostal standards by refraining from tobacco, playing cards, alcohol, dance, and movie theatres. The main focus of the standards was placed on the faculty because they were "the group often most feared by pastors for its education and lack of ministerial credentials and its contact with the vulnerable students" (Corey, 1993, p. 62). Faculty were required to express their agreement and support of the fundamental truths of the Assemblies of God with their own signature on an annual basis.

To complete his terminal degree, Dr. Richard Strahan, the first academic dean at Evangel, focused his dissertation research on the curriculum that would eventually be used to begin Evangel. In it, he states:

> The church has expressed itself openly in declaring it has two special objectives for the college: (1) to perpetuate the atmosphere, traditions, and customs of the church; and (2) to provide opportunity for training for lay people in the activities of the local church (Strahan, 1955, p. vi).

To date, a follow up study to discern whether the university successfully achieved these special objectives has not been conducted. A portion of this study will endeavor to do so.

Strahan (1955) goes on to describe an ideal student for the college as a traditional undergraduate student of 18 years of age, and "ardently religious" living "in a small city" (p.vi). The abstract of his research also details the number of academic departments suggested as well as the student services areas the college would need from the outset (Strahan, 1955). Additionally, Strahan (1955) comments that the college "must develop certain distinctive characteristics if it is to survive and make an outstanding contribution to the clientele it is organized to serve" (p. vii). With a focus on gaining approval and meeting the expectations of the constituents in the General Council, Strahan (1955) describes the expected campus atmosphere as the conclusion to his opening statement regarding development of the college. He states:

> To obtain and maintain the approval of its clientele a campus atmosphere conducive to spiritual and moral development of the individual student must be maintained. Perhaps the most acceptable institution in this respect would be a daily college chapel. Essentially, the atmosphere of the college must be a religious one (Strahan, 1955, p. vii).

Strahan contributes greatly to a foundational understanding of the curriculum and ethos established from the outset at Evangel. His research ranges from the context of the AG's founding and its relationship with education to educational accreditation to the socio-economic conditions of prospective students for Evangel (Strahan, 1955). It bears repeating once more how focused on Pentecostal heritage the early founders of the college were. Strahan details the five objectives outlined by one of the early planning committees for the college in their first meeting. The objectives were:

1. Preserve Pentecostal integrity in the college program.
2. Protect our present Bible Schools.
3. Provide the most effective program.
4. Serve the whole church.
5. Finance the project. (Strahan, 1955, p. 43)

In addition to emphasizing the Pentecostal adherence of the new institution, founders were expecting a successful contribution to Christian higher education in general.

Christian Higher Education

In recent years an increasing emphasis has been placed on researching and understanding the area of academic faith integration in the context of Christian higher education. This has been done through a call for research in a new section of the journal *Christian Higher Education* (Kaak, 2016). A common refrain on Christian college campuses is that all truth is God's truth. Regardless of whether the Bible is quoted or not when truth is taught, it belongs to God (Kaak, 2016). The Christian faith and the academic discipline are required for faith integration to exist. However, faith integration seems to be something more intentional. Hence, the call for more research in this particular area.

Spiritual formation in the university setting has roots in the earliest version of the modern university from the eleventh century church in Paris (Otto & Harrington, 2016). According to a 2011 report from the task force on spiritual formation in Christian higher education created by the Council of Christian Colleges and Universities, spiritual formation can be defined as a biblically guided process in which people are being transformed into the likeness of Christ by the power of the Holy Spirit within the faith community to love and serve God and others (CCCU, 2011). There is a unique and distinctive opportunity on Christian college campuses to work out the purposes of faith in community and explore the relationship between the sacred and the secular across all academic disciplines. "To have a curriculum based on the integration of faith and learning is to pursue God, and Christ, through knowledge" (Otto & Harrington, 2016). Otto and Harrington (2016) ask a crucial question for the Christian liberal arts institution to consider: What is the responsibility to spiritual formation by institutions within Christian higher education? However, considering spiritual formation an institution's responsibility may ultimately damage the attempt for spiritual formation (Wolterstorff et al., 2002). Wolterstorff et al. (2002) believe responsibility evokes thoughts of task, duty, and accountability when, in fact, spiritual formation should be viewed as more of a redemptive process. Furthermore, Otto and Harrington (2016) propose that institutions should increase their focus on the best environment and atmosphere for spiritual development to take place:

> Therefore, the statement that the Christian college has a responsibility for the development of the spiritual formation of its students should be altered in that Christian higher education does not have a specific responsibility to develop the spiritual formation of its students, but rather should focus on creating a distinct and purposeful atmosphere where spiritual formation is promoted and fostered (p. 256).

If spiritual formation and faith integration is a meaningful distinctive for Christian higher education, then it must be determined if those distinctives are changing the outcomes for students and alumni. Schreiner (2018) questions the extent to which CCCU students and alumni are significantly different from their counterparts in other types of universities based on data collected through national surveys. The author emphasizes three frames, or types, of "good" that can come from Christian higher education: individual good, common good, and Kingdom good (Schreiner, 2018).

Individual good includes the personal benefits enjoyed by the student as a result of their enrollment and subsequent graduation from a CCCU institution (Schreiner, 2018). The common good includes benefits for society or the public as a result of an individual's matriculation through a CCCU institution. These benefits include civic engagement, civil discourse, active democracy, global citizens who practice critical thinking, and improvement of overall human well-being (Schreiner, 2018). The third good of Christian higher education is the differentiator for these institutions. The Kingdom good is inclusive of yet transcends both the individual and common good described previously. This final, most distinctive good, includes beliefs and practices that advance the redemptive purposes of the Church and the faith in the world (Schreiner, 2018).

The self-reported research data during the current study indicates alumni of CCCU institutions were highly satisfied with the academic excellence in their preparation, their opportunities to grow intellectually, and reported higher scores in their spiritual development as evidenced by frequency of prayer, scripture reading, and engagement in spiritual disciplines (Schreiner, 2018). Several recommendations for CCCU institutions to thrive in the current environment include:

- Intentionally recruiting mission-aligned students and marketing the distinctive missions which can impact culture
- Develop innovative partnerships which impact the campus and community
- Encourage great campus engagement with the needs of the world
- Orient all faculty, staff, administrators, and students to a growth mindset

- Redesign chapel to better engage the campus community with the global community
- Intentionally connect campus events with opportunities to make a difference

Engage in intellectually and theologically grounded dialogue around current issues such as human sexuality, political and social issues, and ethics in the workplace (Schreiner, 2018)

Clearly, there are many similarities between the program values of Evangel University and the missions of sister institutions within the CCCU. These similarities include an emphasis on the pursuit of truth, developing a strong, biblical foundation for students, and quality academic training and preparation. A more intentional review of the current research relative to the Pentecostal distinctive will follow.

Denominational Identity and Distinctives

Pentecostalism, particularly the AG, is not historically supportive of higher education in general (Corey, 1993). Understanding the healthy tension that exists between the AG and Evangel will help discover opportunities for growth and enhance the ability to expand the mission of the institution. A top-down approach will be used to review the literature surrounding Christian education in general, followed by Evangelicalism, then Pentecostalism more specifically.

Christian Education

Burtchaell (1998) submits a comprehensive analysis of 17 different higher education institutions with roots in Christianity that seemingly left the faith over time. These institutions were affiliated with Congregational, Presbyterian, Methodist, Baptist,

Lutheran, Catholic, Evangelical, and Non-denominational organizations. Burtchaell (1998) presented the founding mission statements of these institutions and tracked the shifting of the mission statements over time along with the corresponding historical events that contributed to those changes. He illuminates the broader cultural events and issues leading to each institution's founding, the challenging early years each institution faced, relationship issues between the board membership and institutional leadership, and battles over funding and finances that were experienced in every story (Burtchaell, 1998). In his analysis, Burtchaell (1998) expressed Christian colleges need a certain level of piety, a strong morality, and meaningful theological discourse to survive and thrive. He also stated, "there is a fourth, catalytic, element in the Christian character of the colleges, one equally needed for their systematic flourishing, and that is the church, a historically continuous community with its own mind and way of life" (Burtchaell, 1998, p. 838).

Glanzer et al. (2019) contested, "Although Burtchaell (1998) argued that a lack of attachment to a denomination places Christian colleges and universities in greater danger to larger, secularizing cultural forces, our study demonstrated different results" (p. 219). However, the Glanzer et al. (2019) study leans heavily on self-reported data as well as in-depth statistical analysis utilizing effect-size thresholds, ANOVA and ANCOVA analyses, and diminishing sample sizes revolving around faculty beliefs and identities. Still, Glanzer et al. (2019) believe their study revealed that a nondenominational identity will not necessarily lead Christian higher education institutions toward the slippery slope of secularization.

Denominations can serve as a strong source of accountability for an institution, but other sources of accountability should also be utilized as appropriate. These sources of accountability include statements of faith, administrator and faculty positions devoted to strengthening the Christian mission, clear hiring requirements, and significant faculty and staff professional development to strengthen their Christian commitment (Glanzer et al., 2019). Clearly, more research is needed to understand the ramifications of a denominational identity compared to a nondenominational identity. Another subtheme includes the very pedagogy in the classroom as the integration of faith and learning takes place.

One of Christian higher education's most distinctive element begins with dedicated Christian faculty members who are experts in their fields and ends with the successful student who demonstrates essential competencies combined with Christlike character (Crider & Crider, 2020). Crider and Crider (2020) contend:

> While we all recognize competency and an ever-developing Christian formation in our students as our ideal end goal, clearly articulated pedagogical frameworks and subsequent functional steps in the formation process seem to be less specific (in the current literature) between the discipline expert (Christian professor) and the final product (student). (p. 34).

Crider and Crider (2020) propose two stages within their model of moving students towards the ideal endpoint with essential competencies and Christlike character. Stage 1 involves a Scripture-based understanding of the discipline while Stage 2 involves what happens in the classroom beginning with relationships. To begin, the authors discuss the challenging presupposition around the common Christian higher education phrase integration of faith and learning (Crider & Crider, 2020). They believe this infers that "faith and learning are two separate, equal subjects to be spliced together like 'art and science' or 'botany and philosophy'" (Crider & Crider, 2020, p. 36). The authors would propose the term faith-informed learning since, in their view, faith should drive learning (Crider & Crider, 2020). An effective Christian higher education pedagogy should be more than a perfunctory prayer to begin a class session. The discipline should be developed from the ground up beginning with the author of the faith who created the discipline (Crider & Crider, 2020).

In Stage 2, the emphasis shifts to relationships. "Education does not occur when students merely think rightly about something. Character formation and competency rely on pedagogy that includes right content and right relationships in the classroom (whether the classroom is on campus or online)" (Crider & Crider, 2020, p. 43). These relationships within the classroom consist of a triune relationship between the course subject or discipline, the professor, and the student. This relationship mirrors the Trinitarian relationship understood in Christianity between God the Father, God the Son, and God the Holy Spirit. This is a key distinctive for Christian higher education. "The dynamic core that renders Christian education extraordinary is a professor who not only models character and competency but also fosters a relational culture in the classroom that gives students a vision of what their future might look like" (Crider & Crider, 2020, p. 46).

Evangelicalism

For centuries, the term *evangelical* has been used to identify churches who promote the gospel message, particularly salvation through faith in Jesus Christ (Hammond, 2019). In the post-Civil War era, churches remained active in their communities, but a belief in the imminent return of Christ led to an increased sense of urgency to *evangelize* and convert unbelievers to faith. At the turn of the 20th century, a growing number of churches began interpreting scripture differently and questioned the absolute truth of scripture while also increasing their efforts for social reform. These beliefs were espoused and expanded in their denominationally-affiliated colleges and seminaries. Those adherents who remained focused on the inerrancy of scripture and the importance of spreading the gospel became known as "fundamentalists."

According to Hammond (2019), "Fundamentalism became the primary identifier for theologically conservative Christians for the first half of the century" (p. 6). Theologically liberal questioning of scripture, emphasis on social reform, and seemingly reduced focus on evangelism was being promoted through the corresponding Christian higher education institutions. As a result, many believers adhering to more "fundamentalist" beliefs became apathetic, distrusting, and even antagonistic towards all higher education in general (Corey, 1993). Still, there were adherents to the evangelical perspective who remained optimistic about the influence of Christian higher education and the prospect of its positive impact on culture. This new evangelical movement perspective grew in popularity around the time Evangel was founded.

One of the earliest proponents of this new evangelical movement was Carl F. H. Henry who used academic arguments to make the case for a progressive fundamentalism. Hammond (2019) notes, "Henry's words were aimed at fundamentalists who were satisfied with building their churches and spreading the gospel message but failed to engage with social issues of the day" (p. 7). Undoubtedly, these were issues with which the AG and its adherents wrestled then and with which they continue to struggle today. Interestingly, this new movement continued to grow around the public ministry and crusades of Billy Graham. His popularity attracted international attention and brought many new adherents to the new evangelical beliefs. His crusades also required much cooperation among local ministers and crossed denominational lines within evangelicalism. The shift towards increased cooperation further differentiated the evangelical movement from fundamentalism (Hammond, 2019). "Through the 1950s, Christian colleges focused their purpose around an evangelical worldview aimed at increased academic quality, accreditation, and liberal arts ideals" (Hammond, 2019, p. 7). That is the precise position where AG leaders found themselves as they forged ahead with the establishment of Evangel College in 1955.

Pentecostal Influence

"Pentecostal theological education is gradually coming into its own, not the least since its seminaries in North America are now in their second generation and accredited at the highest levels" (Yong, 2021, p. 89). While this is true, Pentecostal churches have a well-documented history of anti-intellectualism embedded within their traditions, and this has hindered expansion in higher education altogether (Yong, 2021). As such, there are some, both within the Pentecostal tradition and externally, who would argue that to talk about Pentecost in relationship to theological education would be mixing apples and oranges (Yong, 2021). However, Yong (2021) points out that the earliest believers engaged in theological formation and education through their interaction with the Holy Spirit and each other. For example, Acts 2:42 reads, "They devoted themselves to the apostles' teaching and to fellowship" (The Holy Bible, NIV, 2011). Therefore, a direct connection between the mission of the church and theological education is made from the very beginning of the Christian church.

Yong (2021) emphasizes the importance of unity among the head, the heart, and the hands in the pursuit of a Christian faith. Instead of the historical antagonism between Pentecostal experientialism and higher education, Yong (2021) believes the life in the Spirit involves nurturing and developing the life of the mind and the life of mission together. Long before it was asked, Evangel's founders intended the new liberal arts university would address Yong's (2021) question, "What does theological inquiry, scholarly pursuit, intellectual life, and life of the mind… look like when reconsidered as integral to, rather than disparate from, life in the Spirit?" (p. 98).

Indicators that Set Christian/AG Education Apart
Identifying institutional distinctions is of utmost importance to help justify the increased cost of education for any small private higher education institution (Davis, 2018). For Christian universities to retain their focus and distinctiveness, Davis (2018) points out the necessity to go beyond the usual list of strategic

indicators like finance, enrollment, and academic quality. He argues, "They must instead create and use indicators that are strategic in nature, reporting on how well they are achieving and maintaining distinction in terms of their stated mission" (Davis, 2018, p. 251).

As a result of conducting several rounds of questionnaires with leaders at five different AG institutions, Davis (2018) identifies 28 strategic indicators that feature the distinctiveness of mission for AG higher education institutions. Interestingly, only three indicators were selected for the integration of faith and learning and only two were selected for spiritual formation. According to feedback, more indicators could have been selected if there had been consensus on how to effectively define and measure the integration of faith and learning and spiritual formation. It is interesting to note that Davis' (2018) study involving Pentecostal leaders was unable to identify an agreed upon definition and corresponding metrics for two of the most distinctive objectives of their respective institutions.

Personal Experiences

The personal experiences and stories from alumni and administrators who lived the history of Evangel directly contribute to understanding the context specific to the university Certainly, any histories compiled from administrators who helped lead the university from the outset would be integral to include in this review. Additionally, the experiences of the pioneering students who chose to attend an unknown and paradigm-shifting institution would certainly be important to include. Lastly, the experiences and opinions of leaders who were aware and present during the formation of the institution offer a valuable third-party perspective to consider. When enough of these experiences and histories are collected, common themes begin to emerge that can contribute to an overall understanding of the environment and context from that era of the institution.

These include the following key events that have been referenced by many of the collected histories and experiences:

- First graduation happening only four years after opening
- Accreditation being gained in just one decade
- The first permanent buildings being built
- The beginning of a football program
- The overall spiritual environment and emphasis
- The academic excellence of the founding faculty and subsequently, the depth of career preparation and corresponding success experienced by the earliest alumni.

Summary

As the literature in these areas continues to grow, this study will positively contribute to the conversation about faith integration and spiritual development in higher education by providing historical accounts of how it was successfully achieved at Evangel. Corey (1993) establishes the history of education in the AG leading up to the founding of Evangel, and Strahan (1955) established the specific curriculum and methods to be used to execute the mission of the institution from the outset. This study will attempt to identify whether the mission was successfully carried out over the lives of the earliest alumni.

Denominational distinctives are important to consider to identify how Evangel contributed to the growth of Christian higher education, higher education and evangelicalism, and higher education within Pentecostalism from its beginning. Each subsequent niche of Christianity has a unique relationship with higher education that must be considered.

Finally, the personal experiences of alumni from the first 25 years are an integral aspect to this study. Collected oral and written histories serve as an internal compilation of literature sharing anecdotal evidence of alumni and administrators who experienced the time period being studied firsthand.

The next chapter includes a discussion of the methodology used for this study. The tools and mechanics for collecting the relevant data must be considered to evaluate the reliability and validity of the study. The design of this study relied heavily on interviews and surveys as well as a review of historical documentation.

CHAPTER THREE
RESEARCH DESIGN AND METHODOLOGY

Introduction

Burtchaell (1998) shares that most colleges and universities who originally identified as Christian institutions no longer have a serious, valued, or functioning relationship with the denominations with which they were initially affiliated. For any organization to succeed, there must be an accurate understanding of the founding principles on which it was built. In this qualitative, phenomenological study, a social and historical analysis will be conducted of Evangel University. Evangel is the national university for the leading Pentecostal denomination of the Christian faith, the Assemblies of God (AG). Identifying the important historical landmarks in the first 25 years of Evangel's history will provide an important context for current and future employees and students. This study's qualitative approach utilizes interviews, personal reflections, review of historical documents, and a survey of the experience of students and alumni from the timeframe being studied (1955-1980).

The purpose of this study is to explore by synthesizing common themes derived from firsthand accounts of Evangel alumni, former professors, and administrators who lived the history during the period being studied into a historical narrative. The work builds on Corey's (1993) dissertation and Corey's (2005) historical narrative detailing the founding of the institution. An additional purpose of the collective narrative is to identify events, experiences, and strategies that contributed to the institutional persistence, academic preparation, and flourishing faith integration that characterized the Evangel University experience since its founding in 1955.

Additionally, the study will explore which practices supported the original mission of the university to perpetuate the Pentecostal tradition of the AG through students and to what extent alumni from 1955 through 1980 perceive the commitment to integrate faith and learning impacted their personal and professional lives. Finally, understanding the core ethos of the national university of the AG that was present within the first 25 years and contributed to its successful founding may help determine if the factors discovered can be modernized and intentionally implemented in the current environment and operations at the university.

In this chapter, the research design, methodology, and foundational philosophy of this study are discussed. To successfully accomplish the goals within this research, a qualitative research method will be employed. The lead researcher's foundational pragmatist worldview contributes to the flexibility required to conduct this type of research. Through historical narrative research and phenomenology, a solid understanding of the experiences of alumni, faculty, and staff from the time period studied is established. Taken individually, participants reveal anecdotal evidence of these lived experiences. However, taken collectively and analyzed properly, the compiled information reveals a more comprehensive data set of lived experiences than can be drawn upon and extrapolated for broader application.

Research Questions

The following research questions covering the overarching theme of the study guided the data collection and analysis during this study:

1. How do alumni perceive the spiritual development they experienced while at Evangel University impacted their personal and professional lives?
2. What experiences do alumni, faculty, and staff from the first 25 years share from their time at Evangel?
3. From the perspective of faculty, staff, and alumni, what historical events during the first 25 years of Evangel University's existence shaped the foundational ethos of the institution?
4. Which themes emerge when alumni reflect upon their respective careers and contexts?

Design of the Study

According to Creswell (2014), research design provides specific direction for procedures in data collection and analysis. Qualitative research typically includes narrative research, phenomenological studies, grounded theory, ethnographies, and case studies. This study will utilize grounded theory in a qualitative design leaning heavily on historical narrative research, personal interviews, phenomenology, and surveys.

Creswell (2014) describes an approach to theoretical frameworks within qualitative studies in which establishing a theory becomes the end point. He shares how it is an inductive process of building from the data then moving to broad themes and finally to a generalized model or theory (Creswell, 2014). Grounded theory describes the process by which participants' responses contribute to the development of the study's theoretical framework. Ho and Limpaecher (2022) define grounded theory as "a qualitative method that enables you to study a particular phenomenon or process and discover new theories that are based on the collection and analysis of real-world data" (para. 1).

Lester (1999) states that phenomenological research attempts to describe and explore more than it intends to explain. This is a main function of this research. Phenomenology is attempting to gather a depth of information and perceptions through personal interviews, discussions, and participant observations (Lester, 1999). "Phenomenological studies make detailed comments about individual situations which do not lend themselves to direct generalization in the same way which is sometimes claimed for survey research" (Lester, 1999). For this reason, a survey will attempt to broaden the depth of information collected by interview analysis. It is clear how phenomenology precisely describes the type of research this study is attempting to conduct.

A pragmatic worldview that Creswell (2014) describes as allowing researchers more freedom to select different research methods to fit their needs and purposes molded the methodology for this study. In the case of this study, a pragmatic approach allows for telling the story of multiple individuals who experienced life at the same institution who have multiple experiences, differing perspectives, and a variety of backgrounds. The following sections and subsections provide an overview of the research design and methodology utilized in this study.

Evidence of Sources

Data was collected from multiple sources as part of the researcher's professional responsibilities. During the study, the researcher held the position of Senior Development Officer for University Advancement at Evangel University. Part of his responsibilities included following up with alumni regarding their experiences at Evangel and willingness to continue to support the university. When the researcher's dissertation study proposal was approved, he requested to use the data collected as part of his job and organized it to address the study's research questions.

In addition to firsthand account sources, a review of historical documentation was also conducted. Research from Corey's (1993) work was reviewed as a starting point for the study, and other historical documents were also reviewed.

Human Subjects Protection (RRB)

According to Creswell (2014), the researcher should consider and describe any ethical issues that should be addressed prior to completing the research proposal. In compliance with this guideline, ethical issues that could potentially be a part of this research were properly anticipated. The dissertation advisor was kept informed of the process being used to conduct the research, and the appropriate approval process was used to conduct the research. Permission to conduct the study was requested and granted by the researcher's dissertation committee and the university's Institutional Review Board (IRB). Once these approvals were granted, permission to use already existing data was also granted, and collection of research began. Because the research relied heavily on historical documents and oral histories, any individuals who had been a part of previous interviews sharing historical data and experiences were informed of the potential use of their responses as data for this research. To properly protect participants, no identifying information was used in the final analysis.

Data Collection Procedures

Multiple sources of data were collected and analyzed for this study. One-to-one personal interviews were conducted first. A survey based on interview responses was created to collect additional information. Finally, historical documents including board meeting minutes, press releases, oral histories, and archival documents were perused to glean data to address research questions. Much of the data was collected as part of the researcher's professional responsibilities and permission was sought and granted to use the already existing data from the University.

Identification of Participants

Because of the historical nature of this research, the participants for this study were identified as those individuals who had a meaningful affiliation with Evangel during the timeframe being researched. Some individuals participated in the personal interview stage of the research, some participated in the survey stage of the research, and some participated in both stages.

During the personal interview stage of the research, several longtime faculty and staff members were consulted to develop a preliminary list of personal interview subjects. As interviews began, the final question included a request for recommendations on additional interview subjects. This process yielded a substantial number of additional interview subjects with a broad range of experience and affiliation with the university. This component of the research yielded deeper, more personal feedback and narratives to support the study.

The subsequent survey stage of the research focused primarily on the responses and feedback from alumni who attended Evangel from 1955 through 1980. This included both alumni who graduated and those who did not graduate. This element of the research ensured a broader range of inclusion and response from alumni to expand the study's reach and impact.

Administrators, Faculty, and Staff

Alumni, former administrators, faculty, and staff were mostly involved in the first stage of the research through personal interviews. Their perspectives contributed to the narrative surrounding many of the historical events that took place during the first 25 years of the university. These individuals provided firsthand knowledge and accounts of significant events in the history of the university such as the first graduation, accreditation, the building of the first permanent buildings, chapel and revival experiences, presidential transitions, and the founding of the football program.

Alumni

Alumni from that time period include individuals who attended the university. Graduation during that time period was not a requirement to be included in the study. Most alumni who participated in the personal interview stage of the study did graduate, while some attended during the time period but graduated shortly after 1980. Some alumni interviewed did not graduate at all. Most alumni who contributed to the personal interviews also submitted responses to the subsequent survey. Additionally, some alumni also continued with the university as faculty or staff. Intentional effort was made to encourage responses both through personal interviews and mass surveys that focused on the experience within the time period being studied.

Additional Perspectives

Several participants provided unique additional perspectives that positively contributed to the research. Some were children of leaders and administrators who relived childhood memories from the early years of the university. Others were board members who recollected the discussion and rationale behind significant events like accreditation and presidential transitions. Others were members of other groups who contributed to the formation of the university in the early years like the Laymen's Council and the Women's Auxiliary. From the outset, the Laymen's Council was designed to encourage participation from business-minded men who had the relationships and means to advance the university to stability. The Women's Auxiliary was designed to provide an opportunity for the wives of board members and the Laymen's Council to contribute to the success of the university through prayer, student support, and innovative fundraising efforts.

Description of the Setting

Evangel University is a small, private Christian liberal arts university located in Springfield, Missouri. Evangel is a four year university conferring degrees at all levels, Associates and

Certificates through Ph.D. It is fully-accredited through the Higher Learning Commission with several academic programs also receiving additional national accreditation. Evangel is also the national liberal arts university for the Assemblies of God denomination. As a private higher education institution, it is overwhelmingly tuition-driven in its financial model. Historically, 85-90% of the budget is supported by tuition revenue, thus, the experience of students and satisfaction of alumni is extremely important to sustainable success. Alumni and donor support has continued to climb in recent years, but fundraising efforts met significant challenges in the first 25 years of the institution.

In 1955, there were 93 students who joined the university for its inaugural semester (Cross, 2022). That year ended with 106 total students as 13 joined for the Spring semester. In the 25 years that followed, there was consistent and significant growth. In the fall of 1980, the institution saw its largest class of new students in its history to that point, and even since then, with 760 new students joining for the Fall of 1980. That school year (1980-81) ended with a total of 1,851 students, culminating this 25-year period with the largest enrollment to that point in history. This growth only included traditional undergraduate students as graduate and online programs did not begin until years after this time period. Evangel's current enrollment is 2,367. See Appendix A for the full enrollment report for 1955 – 1980.

Data Collection Instruments

Qualitative methods for data collection included one-to-one personal interviews to establish the participants' foundational experiences. Additionally, a survey was used to provide additional information regarding participant experiences. Although most data were collected prior to the study, a description of the data collection instruments and protocols for data collection are provided below.

One-to-One Interviews – Instrument

Interviewees included alumni, former administrators, former faculty, and former staff members, and their experiences ranged across the time period being researched. The interview questions were developed by the researcher. They began with personal interviews of individuals who had experience at the university within the first 25 years of the university's existence. Interview responses were used to address each research question.

The original mission of the university was to perpetuate the Pentecostal traditions of the AG through the next generation of students. Seventeen questions were prepared to glean information about the participants' current situation and their experiences at Evangel in the past. Several interview questions were intended to determine if the mission was achieved in the university's first 25 years. Others were used to further discern whether or not the Pentecostal traditions were perpetuated unrelated to the specific AG denomination. The remainder of the questions collected information regarding the participants' perceptions of the university's strengths, challenges, and effectiveness as well as demographic information and the participants' reasons for coming to Evangel. The questions used for the personal interviews are included in Appendix B.

One-to-One Interview Protocol

Interviewees were located throughout the world and identified with the use of the university's alumni database. Participants for interviews were selected based on recommendations from individuals with strong historical knowledge of the institution, the researcher's experience with participants, as well as pre-recorded interviews and oral histories already available in the archives of the university. Potential interviews were set up via email. Interviews were conducted in person and recorded utilizing a handheld recording device, and in some cases when there was distance between the researcher and interviewee, a video conferencing tool was used to record the discussion. In other instances, the interviews were conducted via phone call, and the handheld recording device was used while the phone call was on the speaker phone setting. This was done for interviewees who were not comfortable with using the video conferencing tool. Interviews were transcribed to transfer the oral histories into written form and more easily identify the major themes present throughout the study. This allowed for a high level of precision when coding and identifying themes from the interviews.

During administration of in-person interviews, a comfortable setting was chosen based on the participants preference. Clear instruction was given that interviews would be recorded, and questions to guide the interview were given prior to the scheduled time of the interview for proper preparation by the participant. Interviews typically lasted between 60-90 minutes and interviewees were sent an email explaining the intent of the interview. They were also informed that the interview would be recorded and that responses would be kept anonymous. A copy of a version of the email that was sent to interview participants can be found in Appendix C. These interviews also served a purpose of important data collection and relationship building as part of the researcher's primary work at the university. The researcher was authorized to utilize this and other interview data for research purposes for this study. The participants were also informed of the uses of their interview responses once the research proposal was approved.

Participant Survey - Instrument

A survey was created from the interview responses to collect further information related to themes that emerged from the interviews. For the corresponding survey, an expert statistician was consulted in developing the survey questions to establish a high level of reliability and validity across the survey questions. All survey correspondence was sent via email. Responses were collected using an online survey tool. Utilizing this approach made analyzing the data and responses more efficient.

Survey questions were designed to explore alumni perceptions of their personal faith prior to attending Evangel, during their time as students at Evangel, immediately after graduating from Evangel, and now. Responses to the questions address Research Questions 3 and 4 regarding alumni perspectives of their spiritual development and how Evangel may have impacted that development. Additionally, the survey was designed to explore a more comprehensive perception from alumni about their experience at Evangel during the first 25 years. Questions ranged from being open-ended to using a Likert scale to assess perceptions. The survey also endeavored to identify personnel who made positive impacts on student perceptions during that time in the hopes that the researcher could follow up with the most named individuals to explore how they were effective in their work. A full list of the survey questions used is in Appendix D.

Participant Survey – Protocol

The survey was sent to all alumni across the 25-year period being researched along with multiple reminders. Email addresses of alumni who fit this demographic were identified through the alumni database in the Evangel University Advancement office. Appropriate instruction and consent information was shared via email and in the introduction to the survey to properly inform survey participants of the purpose of the survey and how the information obtained would be used. Appendix E includes emails used to invite potential survey respondents to participate. Demographic data requested in the survey allowed for disaggregation of responses by gender, location, major, and graduation year.

Historical Document Data Collection

To begin this historical analysis for the institution, a review of important documents from the first 25 years was conducted. This involved researching all available documentation available in the university archives from 1955 to 1980. These documents included charter documents, board minutes, academic program files, other historical narratives, research collected and conducted by Corey, oral histories from key personnel in leadership as well as documents in the Flower Pentecostal Heritage Center at the Assemblies of God National Office. Some of those documents were available on site and some in their online collection.

Data Analysis

Data analysis began with the transcription of recorded interviews. Additionally, survey responses were charted and categorically analyzed to further identify themes that emerged from the interview responses. Lester (1999) suggests the use of mind maps and word maps to assist in coding of interviews for phenomenological research like this. Finally, review of the data collected from historical documents was triangulated with interview and survey responses by comparing interview responses with responses gathered through surveys. Appendix F provides an example of how this was done to identify major themes.

One-to-One Interview Data Analysis

All the personal interviews were recorded and transcribed. Transcriptions were subjected to electronic word searches to identify common phrases and ideas expressed most during the interviews. As patterns developed, emergent themes were identified and survey questions were designed to collect similar objective data from a larger sample of the target population.

Participant Survey Data Analysis

Once the survey data was collected, analysis was done to reveal trends in the experiences and perceptions of the respondents. The information compiled was compared against the interview responses to confirm the experiences of the larger group of alumni at scale. Information was also gathered to identify what elements of the experiences in the first 25 years may be incorporated into the future strategic planning for the university. Survey data was also compared to the historical documents and information available in the archives of the university to add anecdotal and subjective material representing the real experiences of alumni. As responses to interviews and surveys were collected, these subjective experiences were overlayed with objective data like enrollment, campus development projects, budget issues, and other key events that may be connected to the experiences of the participants.

Historical Document Data Analysis

From the analysis of historical documents, a list of key events, such as gaining accreditation, presidential transitions, building permanent buildings, and launching a football program, from the first 25 years of the university was compiled. The list was then compared to the interview and survey responses to identify how key events may have contributed to the growth of the university and the execution of the mission of the university during its founding years.

Role of the Researcher

Most of the interview data for this study was collected by the researcher in his role as Senior Development Officer for University Advancement at Evangel University. After receiving approval to use the previously existing data, the researcher served as the analyzer of the data. Creswell (2014) states that, pertaining to qualitative research, researchers should explicitly identify their biases that shape their interpretations formed during the study. The researcher had several transformational experiences while involved as a student and employee at the university being researched. These experiences include successfully obtaining a bachelor's and master's degree, finding employment at the university immediately upon graduation, and meeting his future spouse while a student at the university. While several attempts were made to remain unbiased during the research, because of these experiences, it was difficult to completely remove all bias from the analysis conducted during this research.

Trustworthiness

To ensure trustworthiness of this study, several steps were taken by the researcher. The researcher acknowledges the personal biases that may impact the interpretations of the study. Efforts were made throughout the study to reduce the impact of the personal biases of the researcher. These efforts included a comprehensive exploration of the experiences of alumni and administrators who were interviewed. This was done by including questions to address any weaknesses or shadow areas of the university during the time period being studied. Interviewees were asked to share any knowledge or experiences they had that might reflect a weakness or shortcoming of the university during their time. After these questions were asked, healthy discussion ensued to ensure the study was discovering all aspects of the university's earliest experiences.

The interviews were recorded and saved prior to transcription so the accuracy of the transcription could be verified. The transcriptions were reviewed and analyzed to identify the common themes and topics discussed that assisted in the development of the mass survey sent to all alumni from the time period being studied. All feedback in interviews and surveys was requested directly from the individuals who were present at the university during the time period being studied. These were first-person accounts which maximized the number of primary sources utilized in the development of the historical narrative component of the study.

Dr. Jeff Fulks is a research expert who was consulted to ensure data was analyzed correctly and collected properly. As the survey was developed from the interview transcripts and recordings, this research expert verified the accuracy of the questions which were developed.

Summary

This study will provide a comprehensive assessment of the foundational years of Evangel University and their impact on the students and alumni over the course of their careers and lives. This data will be utilized to better equip leaders to intentionally implement the unique methods and procedures of excellent academic preparation, spiritual development, and faith integration which were successful in the early years for Evangel. As such, it is important the methodology of the study is carefully sequenced and accurately executed.

The research questions utilized for the personal interviews were asked across the range of interviews that were conducted. Minor adjustments were made depending on if the individual was a former student, administrator, faculty member, or staff member. The more than 40 personal interviews conducted provided a strong foundation for the development of the survey that was sent to 1,652 alumni via email.

Participants were informed of the intent of the personal interviews and the mass survey following appropriate protections and procedures guidelines. Permission was granted from each participant prior to conducting the interviews, and they were informed that the conversations would be recorded. Additionally, the role of the researcher in the study has been appropriately disclosed along with any biases that may have been present.

In the subsequent sections of this study, the research findings will be presented and interpreted along with the historical narrative of the time period being studied.

CHAPTER FOUR
A HISTORICAL NARRATIVE OF THE FIRST 25 YEARS OF EVANGEL UNIVERSITY

Introduction

On June 30, 1955, the official Articles of Agreement of Evangel College of the Assemblies of God were signed by the founding president, Klaude Kendrick, the first secretary of the board of trustees, Harold F. Gray, and the first business manager, Roy Ditto ([Article of Agreement], 1955). Later, on August 22, 1955, the articles were officially filed with the State of Missouri ([Articles of Agreement], 1955). As such, Evangel University began its existence as a recognized entity of higher education.

Corey (1993) mentions the tightrope that was walked by the founders of Evangel, predominantly Rev. Ralph Riggs, who endeavored to perpetuate the Pentecostal traditions of the Assemblies of God and expand access to higher education training to young people pursuing areas outside of vocational ministry. As if to confirm the existence of this invisible tightrope, the preamble of Evangel states:

> Under Divine Providence the Assemblies of God has enjoyed a phenomenal growth and development. In the Year of our Lord 1953, the Twenty-fifth General Council of the Assemblies of God in session in Milwaukee, Wisconsin, recognized the need of establishing a Senior College Program and adopted necessary legislation.
>
> Therefore, the Evangel College of the Assemblies of God shall be as a unit of this program founded for the purpose of providing a *Christian college for the training of youth in a Pentecostal atmosphere where the arts and sciences and such specialized courses as may be adopted* by its Board of Directors shall be taught. ([Articles of Agreement], 1955, Preamble, emphasis added)

Later in article two, section one of these same articles, it states:

> The General Council, and General Presbytery of the Assemblies of God are charged to be the guardians of this institution to see that it promotes forever the ideals and purposes for which it is founded in the year of our Lord 1955, and *is directed to take whatever steps necessary to insure purity of doctrine and excellence of scholarship.* ([Articles of Agreement], 1955, Article 2, Section 1, emphasis added).

With a campus established, qualified faculty hired, and legal paperwork crystallizing the expectations of the General Council formalized, Evangel was prepared to accept its first class of 93 students and begin operation. Throughout the course of the first 25 years of Evangel's existence, so much was dependent upon the leadership abilities of the presidents who were in place. There will always be more that can be stated when attempting to compile a historical narrative about any organization, especially one as complex, dynamic, and expansive as a higher education institution. As such, this narrative will focus on the tenures and leadership styles of the three presidents who lead the institution during the first 25 years. This does not include Rev. Ralph Riggs, who could be considered the president of Evangel while it only existed as an idea. His role in the establishment and operation of Evangel cannot be overstated. Many have shared and agree that he essentially sacrificed his career to see Evangel take flight (Kendrick, 1980; Riggs, 1969).

While focusing on the three presidents during this time period, a review of each inauguration celebration and message, key points during their tenure, and their subsequent resignations will be made. This, along with the experience of faculty, staff, and students from this era, will reveal emerging themes that deeply impacted the ethos of the institution as it is understood today. A certain "underdog mentality" pervaded the experience, actions, and belief systems of the founding years that resulted in many displays of self-sacrificial leadership at all levels.

Additionally, the political elements that were prevalent from the beginning must be considered. Government politics played integral roles in acquiring the property for the campus, receiving federal financial aid and funding, and eventually receiving the coveted regional accreditation. Organizational politics also played key roles over the years as the institution and its leaders navigated the relationship with the Assemblies of God and corresponding constituencies. Bolman and Deal (2013) have much to say about the political frame of an organization.

According to Bolman and Deal (2013) politics is the realistic process of making decisions and allocating resources in a context of scarcity and diverging interests. This certainly describes the context within which the leaders of Evangel and the AG were working to establish the first Pentecostal liberal arts institution in the country. The financial challenges that were present along with the diverging interests of what the college should accomplish created a political ecosystem only the shrewdest leaders could navigate.

Lastly, for continuity and full understanding of the context underlying the first 25 years of existence, a thorough review should be made of Corey's (1993) work that sets the stage leading up to the operational history of Evangel.

Dr. Klaude Kendrick Presidency (1955 – 1958)

A full bio of Dr. Kendrick's career is appropriate to include to provide context for the spiritual depth and academic strength that was identified in Dr. Kendrick to become the founding president of Evangel. Dr. Klaude Kendrick had the distinction of having served as president of three Assemblies of God institutions of higher education. In addition to his service to Evangel, he later became president of Southwestern Assemblies of God University, 1960-1965; and Asia Pacific Theological Seminary, Philippines, 1984-86.

Dr. Kendrick was a 1938 graduate of Southwestern Assemblies of God University. He also earned a B.A. from Texas Wesleyan College, an M.A. from Texas Christian University, and a Ph.D. in history from the University of Texas. His book titled *The Promise Fulfilled* is a complete scholarly history of the modern Pentecostal movement.

Dr. Kendrick served Southwestern Assemblies of God University as an instructor, dean of men, business manager, and vice president from 1940 to 1955. He was a member of the

Educational Committee that reported to the General Council meeting in Milwaukee in 1953. It was this report, accepted by the General Council, that resulted in the founding of Evangel College. He then became the founding president of Evangel and served Evangel for two additional years as academic dean. The Klaude Kendrick Library at Evangel University and Kendrick Hall at Southwestern Assemblies of God University are named for him.

During his time at Evangel, Dr. Kendrick recruited an exceptionally strong faculty. In his second year as president, 1956-57, with Evangel only two years old, Evangel's academic program was recognized by the University of Missouri Committee on Accredited Schools. In his first year as academic dean of Evangel, Missouri Teacher certification was granted to Evangel, with other states granting reciprocity. At the end of the same year, 1958-59, Evangel's first senior class was graduated.

Dr. Kendrick left Evangel in 1960 to assume the presidency of Southwestern Assemblies of God University. In 1965 he resigned to become Chairman of the Division of Social Sciences at Texas Wesleyan College. He remained at Texas Wesleyan until 1977, and then accepted the position of Academic Dean of Southern California College. He returned to Southwestern in 1981 as professor of history, government and sociology. He retired in 1983, but came out of retirement in 1984 to become president of Asia Pacific Theological Seminary (then named FEAST), serving as a missionary volunteer.

An ordained minister of the Assemblies of God, Dr. Kendrick has pastored churches in Arkansas, California, Kansas, and Texas. He also served the North Texas District as sectional presbyter and executive presbyter.

Dr. Kendrick married Grace Bogan, and they became parents of two children, Karen and Carl. After Grace's death, he married his second wife, Mable. In addition to his academic and pastoral ministry, he served as a Director of the Christian Fidelity Life Insurance Company.

On December 28, 1954, roughly nine months before the inaugural fall semester was supposed to begin, Klaude Kendrick was formally announced as the founding president of Evangel College. Interestingly, J. Robert Ashcroft, the second president of Evangel, was also a member of that committee as Education Secretary for the Assemblies of God. According to Ashcroft (1988), committee meetings in May of 1954 saw Kendrick put forth as a candidate by Ralph Riggs, enthusiastically selected, and unanimously approved to become the founding president. He was 37 years old when he was selected and 38 when he officially took office.

Prior to officially beginning his tenure as president, Kendrick was already displaying the self-sacrificial leadership that would come to characterize each of the three presidents during the time period being studied. In a letter dated September 11, 1954, J. Robert Ashcroft, who was serving as Education Secretary for the Assemblies of God at that time, provided an update to Kendrick, who was still working full-time as a professor at Southwestern Bible College. In this letter, Ashcroft reveals several key points regarding the progress of the development of Evangel. Most specifically to Kendrick, he shares:

> Brother Kendrick, it disturbs me a great deal that I have not been able to find a way or an authorization to forward you the remittance which was decided upon by the Board

of Directors. I have discussed this problem with Brother Scott, Brother Riggs, and other members of the Board of Directors, and they have recommended, facing the situation squarely, that there seemed to be no alternative but to ask you if you would be so kind as to give us a moratorium. (Ashcroft, 1954, p. 1).

In the foregoing sections of the same letter, Ashcroft indicates there has been little progress related to the bulletin, later known as the academic catalog, of the developing institution. He also states, "...time is going by with such rapidity that I am fearful that we will not be able to complete our plans for the dollar-per-member drive in time for the Thanksgiving-Christmas period" (Ashcroft, 1954, p. 1). It happened that the first official fundraising attempt would not materialize, and Kendrick would begin the work as founding president without a paycheck.

Nevertheless, the spring of 1955 saw copious amounts of letters and correspondence from Kendrick as he moved wholeheartedly into the recruitment of faculty to join Evangel. Some of those key faculty who were recruited during the presidency of Klaude Kendrick include Edna Baker, Frances Berkihiser, Nonna Dalan, Steve Davidson, Walter Ernst, June Kean, Don Pearson, Thurman Vanzant, and Grace Walther ([Notes from Klaude Kendrick], 1988). Interestingly, many of these names are also mentioned in alumni interviews and alumni surveys when respondents are asked to share names of influential faculty members. The spiritual leadership and academic strength of the first group of faculty members were unique and uncommon for a startup institution and contributed much to establishing a firm foundation of operation and mission execution.

As spring gave way to summer, the AG leaders and school administrators were sprinting toward the launch of Evangel College. In June of 1955, an open house was hosted for the Springfield community to see the campus of this new institution for the first time. Later that same month, the founding articles of agreement were signed, and they were officially filed in August just 17 days before the inauguration of Klaude Kendrick as president and just nine days before the very first freshmen orientation on September 1, 1955. Classes officially began on Tuesday, September 6, 1955.

Inauguration

In the afternoon of September 8, 1955, Evangel College celebrated the inauguration of the very first president in its history, Klaude Kendrick. Gaining accreditation was top of mind for Riggs as he initially invited the Associate Secretary for the North Central Association of Colleges and Secondary Schools (NCACSS), Manning M. Pattillo, to be the inauguration speaker (Pattillo, 1955). The NCACSS was the main regional accrediting association for Evangel. Pattillo was scheduled to be in Eastern Canada during that time and politely declined with a statement that read in part, "I have watched the development of the College from the very beginning, and I would really enjoy being present at the inauguration of your first president" (Pattillo, 1955, p. 1).

Nevertheless, the inauguration for Kendrick moved forward successfully with the well-known Senator of Missouri's 7th District, The Honorable Dewey Short, delivering the inaugural address. Sen. Short played a significant role in the land acquisition needed for Evangel to have a campus. At that time, leaders with the AG were very active in the Springfield community, particularly Thomas F. Zimmerman and J. Roswell Flower. As attempts were being made to acquire the O'Reilly property, Zimmerman had a meeting with local business leader Lester Cox. Mr. Cox owned Burge Hospital which went on to become the hospital at Cox North, a part of the major Cox Health Hospital System in Southwest Missouri. When hearing about the challenges the AG was having in moving the application for the property forward, Cox called Sen. Short while Zimmerman was in his office. They spoke for about 20 minutes, and from that time on, the application proceeded successfully while Sen. Short made it his personal mission to see it through (Zimmerman, 1988). In an oral history collected and transcribed by the longtime Evangel University archivist, Betty Chase, Charles Scott shares his perspective of Sen. Short. Charles Scott was a member of the Education committee and attended both planning meetings after the General Council approved the development of a Senior College Program at the 1953 General Council in Milwaukee. He went on to serve as the very first chairman of the Board of Trustees for Evangel. He shared that Sen. Short just so happened to be the minority chairman of the House Military Affairs Committee while the AG was attempting to acquire the property. There are many providential coincidences like this sprinkled throughout the history of Evangel. Scott goes on to state.

> The officials of the General Services Administration had expressed their intention of selling the O'Reilly Hospital for the highest market price, that would bring possibly up to three million dollars. But Mr. Short objected to this procedure and stated, 'The dedicated young people who will be graduated from a college like this will be of far more

value to the United States than the three million dollars we might get by selling the property.' (Scott, 1963, p. 4) When considering the alumni who matriculated through Evangel in the first 25 years, history shows Mr. Short was overwhelmingly correct.

"Congressman Dewey Short, guest speaker at the opening ceremonies, predicted that by 1960 the new college will have an enrollment of 1,000" (Evangel, 1955, p. 6). Later correspondence between Riggs and Ashcroft would strike a celebratory tone confirming the prediction of Sen. Short. Riggs (1969) states, "I was glad to know that your enrollment now approaches 1000. You will remember that this is what Congressman Short predicted at the time of the dedication, about 15 years ago." As the very first pioneer of the idea of Evangel, Riggs exhibited significant self-sacrificial leadership to see the college established to the detriment of his own career.

During the inauguration of Klaude Kendrick, Bro. Scott, as chairman of the board, delivered the very first presidential charge. In it, he states, "I do not hesitate to charge you first of all – with the care of the spiritual life of the students – of the faculty – and everyone connected with the College" (Scott, 1955, p. 2). Additionally, Scott charged Kendrick to maintain a "…high academic level, together with proper spiritual emphasis…" (Scott, 1955, p. 3). With potential prophetic implications, Scott also shares expectations for Kendrick "…to defend the freedom and democracy of our great country – by your faithful presentation of TRUTH which is the greatest influence in neutralizing the ideologies which are seeking to destroy our freedom and democratic way of life" (Scott, 1955, p. 3). A final call to remembrance touches on one of the core beliefs that has been carried out at Evangel from the beginning, and perhaps this statement in the inaugural charge to the president is a reason why. Scott states, "And remember, these students are not for the school – but the school is for these students" (Scott, 1955, p.4).

As a staunch academic rooted in the Assemblies of God, Kendrick brought a unique perspective with him as he served as the founding president. In his inaugural address to the Chamber of Commerce for the city of Springfield, he introduced Evangel to the business community with gratitude and promised a collaboration and indebtedness to the city for the assistance its leaders provided to the founding of Evangel. He also said, "…I am convinced that the growth of the college will be limited only by the vision and resources of those who are in a position to assist its development" (Kendrick, 1955, p. 5).

An explanation of the college curriculum at Evangel taken from the inauguration program explains the type of experience and programs that will be offered at Evangel.

> Evangel College, while providing a wholesome general education, will also prepare Assemblies of God youth to enter careers in…
>
> BUSINESS: Opportunity keeps its door open to individuals who are prepared to pursue careers in business, accounting, secretarial science, and business education.
>
> EDUCATION: Daily the shortage of elementary and secondary school teachers becomes more acute. The classroom provides an outstanding challenge for those who are seeking a place of Christian service.
>
> SCIENCE: The demand for college graduates trained in science and mathematics is greater than the supply. Young

men and women specializing in these fields may well find themselves on the brink of promising careers.

MUSIC: Performers, church music directors, and public school music teachers will find that Evangel College provides good training as well as a variety of opportunities for expression for those with musical talent.

NURSING: As a career, nursing provides an unusual opportunity for service. Missions, private nursing, public health, and education beckon to the professionally trained nurse.

Evangel College has an academically prepared faculty who have a definite spiritual interest in their students thus providing an unusual educational opportunity (The College Curriculum, 1955, p. 1).

During the startup festivities, on September 9, 1955, Dean Strahan shared a report with the Board of Directors "…that the faculty recommends that the following school colors and mascot or slogan be presented for consideration:

School colors – maroon and white

School mascot or slogan – Crusaders

A motion to receive the Dean's report carried" ([Faculty Meeting Minutes], 1955, p. 1)

Faculty moved, seconded, and passed a motion for the school colors and mascot in a faculty affairs meeting on August 30, 1955, a few days before the board report by Dean Strahan.

Operations of the College

From the beginning, financial challenges have been present for the institution. The tuition charge when Evangel opened in 1955 was just $10 per semester hour. Accounting for an average of

3.6% annual inflation, that would be equivalent to $110.75 in 2023. This is still very low for an institution whose budget is predicated on tuition fees. While the academic fortitude of the faculty was strong from the outset and the enrollment trends of the first twenty-five years were impressive for a startup university, finances played a significant role in each presidential transition of this time period.

Though his tenure was brief, the enrollment trend during Kendrick's time as president showed growth each year, as is indicated in Figure 1.

Figure 1

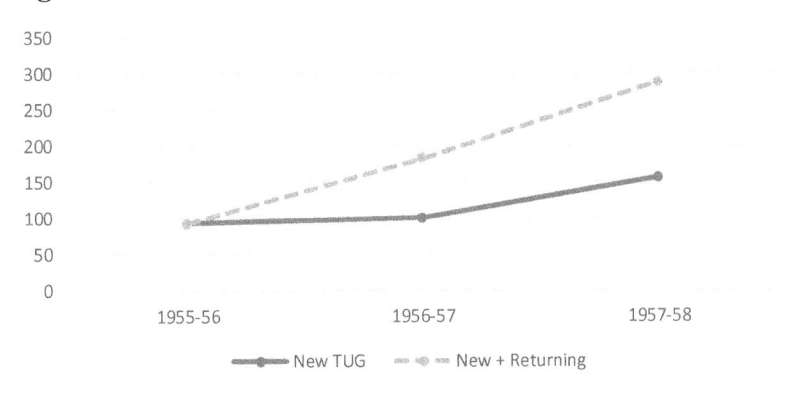

Kendrick Presidency Enrollment Trend

It should also be stated that the president of a university is not solely responsible for enrollment. There are many other personnel within a properly functioning higher education institution who bare the main responsibility of growing enrollment. Additionally, external circumstances also can significantly impact the enrollment trends of a university. However, the president must ultimately answer to the board of trustees when it comes to enrollment issues.

A secondary funding mechanism for a university is related to fundraising activities. Figure 2 visualizes the trends of funding that came from contributions and tuition income and includes the trend for total income. Contributions can also be understood to mean donations. The Assemblies of God did provide grant funding to the institution from 1960-61 through 1978-79, and those grants are included in the contributions data. Tuition income indicates the amount of income that came to the university from tuition and direct student fees. Not included in tuition income is auxiliary income that includes revenues from items like room, meal plans, snack shop revenues, rental property income, and other items not directly attributed to tuition and student fees. This also explains the gap between contributions, tuition income, and total income. Total income combines all sources of revenue for the institution. The enrollment trend, tuition per hour costs, and income trend graphs are included for each president's tenure along with a full 25-year trend for each item in the summary.

Kendrick does not have a tuition per hour cost graph because the tuition cost per hour during his presidency was $10 for his first two years and $12 for his third and final year. Contributions, tuition income, and total income data was taken from the audited financial reports available in the Evangel University Business and Finance Office Vault. The purpose of these figures is to reveal the fiscal and fiduciary management of the institution during each president's tenure.

Figure 2

```
$350 000,00
$300 000,00                                    ●
$250 000,00
$200 000,00                    ●
$150 000,00
$100 000,00    ●
 $50 000,00
         $-
            1955-56         1956-57         1957-58
         ●—All Contributions  ●—Tuition Income  ●●●Total Income
```

Kendrick Presidency - Contributions, Enrollment Income, Total Income

As previously referenced, one of the first major fundraising efforts did not materialize as anticipated by the committee developing the Senior College Program. The gift of the campus from the federal government may have resolved the location of college, but it did not alleviate budget concerns the way many assumed it would. In an interview with J. Robert Ashcroft, Education Secretary for the AG during Kendrick's presidential tenure, and eventually the second president of Evangel, indicated the O'Reilly property not costing the AG or Evangel any money proved to be a fallacy (Ashcroft, 1988). Understood in his comments were the costs associated with renovating the campus and updating and furnishing the buildings that would be used being overlooked. He states:

> Well, one thing that I guess was characteristic, we really didn't count the cost and know what it was going to entail financially to have a college. We were all flying by the seat of our pants, if I can use that expression, and I think it was traditional of the Assemblies of God to start something up without really doing enough financial research to know what it was going to cost.

We really don't know yet what it's going to cost to do a lot of things. We go ahead and do it. I remember attending a meeting where it was said, 'Oh, boy, don't ask what it is going to cost because if we do that, we might not decide to do what we ought to be doing, so let's do what we ought to do and then try to find out how to finance it afterwards.' (Ashcroft, 1988, p. 5-6)

Compounding this underlying sentiment related to financing, Corey (1993) revealed how Ralph Riggs made a statement indicating that Evangel would not utilize any money from the General Council. This statement was widely spread and became an understanding of the constituency. Perhaps the statement was made in an effort to push the authorization to start Evangel across the finish line, or perhaps it was made as hyperbole and Riggs intended to mean Evangel might utilize some funding but not enough to be detrimental to the AG. Whichever the case, that statement proved not to be the reality, may have subverted some of the initial public support that was garnered for the institution, and really did not follow the precedent that was set for the Bible colleges which preceded Evangel.

In a letter from Betty Chase (1990) to former President Ashcroft, she informs him that she had unearthed information showing substantial subsidies from the General Council for Central Bible Institute. Apparently, this information was not well-known across the constituency. According to General Council minutes, subsidies from the General Council and the Gospel Publishing House were made for Central Bible Institute in 1925, 1929, 1933 and referenced in 1939 (Chase, 1990). "The 1925 report shows that nearly half of CBI's income from 1923 to 1925 was in the form of these subsidies" (Chase, 1990, p. 1).

Clearly, there was precedent for significant financial assistance from the General Council. However, according to multiple oral histories and interviews with leaders from that time, soliciting financial assistance or even assistance to develop their own financial support would prove to be a challenge for early Evangel administrators.

Corey (1993) covered the failed efforts at fundraising the General Council did attempt on behalf of Evangel, and both Kendrick and Ashcroft expressed the challenges they experienced in gaining any sort of financial support from the General Council in the early years. One way many institutions can gather needed funding is through short-term financing programs to get through lean parts of the year, like summertime. The challenge for Evangel at that time was there was no history on which to rely for collateral (Ashcroft, 1988). This presented another financial challenge for Evangel to have to rely on the General Council for a sort of co-sign for this financing (Ashcroft, 1988). Related to the challenges of gaining more direct sources of funding from the General Council, Ashcroft expresses it this way:

> Well, I think there were joint meetings of the Executive Presbytery and the Finance Committee. There was a lot of interchange of ideas like this [on how to address lack of finances]. It was a traumatic experience. It was so traumatic that it led to some desperate action. I went to Brother Riggs, and I said, 'We just have to have better communication with the denomination. We are unable to use the mailing list of the Pentecostal Evangel, we are unable to use the mailing list of Men's Fellowship, we are unable to use the mailing list of Revivaltime, we are unable to use the mailing list of the WMC (Women's Missionary Council), we are unable to use Revivaltime as an appeal for students or for money.' So we

were kind of blocked off from every line of communication, and one of the things that I did at that time was to establish the magazine. We couldn't use the Pentecostal Evangel; we couldn't use the other publications in order to communicate. We had no lines of communication. Of course, that gave rise to the suggestion I gave to Brother Riggs about the Evangel College Council. 'We need communication. How do we get it? If we don't go through the pastor, how do we get it? Well, we go through laymen.' So that gave rise to the College Council and the Ladies Auxiliary. (Ashcroft, 1988, p. 4).

Once Bro. Riggs authorized Ashcroft's idea to form the Evangel College Advisory Council, he wrote to hundreds of laymen across the country who might be good members. This group's intent was to inform and advise the leadership of the institution on business items and building projects while also providing financial resources. Considering the Board of Trustees was required to be made up of mostly pastors according to the by-laws, and that the Board of Trustees is traditionally where much of the most significant fundraising efforts occur, the Evangel College Council filled a huge financial gap for the institution. According to Ashcroft, "So we brought those [Council members] in, and bang! There's where we got started on our library, the gymnasium, the dormitories, the cafeteria, remodeling. The whole ball of wax probably came out of the Advisory Council idea" (Ashcroft, 1988, p. 17). The members of the Evangel College Council facilitated much of the growth Evangel experienced in the first 25 years. Interestingly, after seeing the success the Council had for Evangel, many of the other AG Bible schools began their own versions of them as well.

Still, as year two turned to year three, there was a looming financial crisis brewing because of the roughly $300,000 debt that had been accumulated and unresolved from the founding years. Evangel was forced to go back to the General Council and consider all options to address this debt while keeping the operations of the institution running. This is where another significant show of self-sacrificial leadership was displayed as Dr. Kendrick and Dr. Strahan both put the benefit of the institution, and ultimately the students, above themselves. Dr. Kendrick would lean heavily on assistance from Secretary Ashcroft to address this financial crisis. As Education Secretary, Ashcroft was intricately involved with the financial development of the school, specifically working as the chairman of the finance committee in the institution's early development. In 1957, a fundraiser for all of the higher education institutions was attempted. To avoid a show of favoritism, all schools were invited to participate in a national College Day Giving program the national office sponsored. The report from Ashcroft begins with the statement, "Progress is being made, though exceedingly slowly, in establishing a College Day emphasis among our constituents" ([College Day Giving report], 1957, p. 1). Ashcroft admits his office was unable to tabulate all of the funds the schools that participated had received directly, but he does share what the Education Department received in response to a two-page center spread and cover of the March 17, 1957 issue of the *Pentecostal Evangel*. It should be noted, the *Pentecostal Evangel* was a national, weekly publication sent to all AG churches in the United States that helped communicate important information with the constituency. Many students surveyed and interviewed for this research indicated having heard about Evangel through this publication. The results published in Ashcroft's report were as follows:

Not allocated to any school - $103.11
Designated to Evangel College - $37.82
Designated to Southeastern - $12.00
Designated to Southwestern   - $76.00
Total - $228.93 ([College Day Giving report], 1957, p. 1).

The results from this effort reveal how remarkable the continued growth and development of the institution were. Some would say it was miraculous and divinely inspired.

Accreditation was another major part of the early development at Evangel, and Dr. Kendrick understood one of his major assignments to be the pursuit of accreditation from the very first semester. The successful beginning of the accreditation process may be considered Dr. Kendrick's most important contribution to the founding of Evangel. In the very first year of existence, Dr. Kendrick and the academic dean, Dr. Richard Strahan, visited the headquarters of the North Central Association of Colleges and Secondary Schools in Chicago. They were rebuffed because of a lack of historical existence and told there was no assistance or study program that could be given to guide them to accreditation at that time (Kendrick, 1963). Frustrated and dejected, they began their trip back to Evangel. What happened next could be considered another providential coincidence in the development of Evangel:

> On our way home we [came] by the way of Columbia, Missouri and visited with those persons at the University who were responsible for the accrediting of junior colleges on the state level in the state of Missouri. We discussed our problem with Dr. Townsend, who was then dean of the College of Education, explaining that we desired only a high-quality educational program and certainly desired to

make as few mistakes as possible, and sought desperately the best direction and guidance we could receive. He, as a consequence, called together the appropriate persons from the staff of the University, explained our situation and desire, asked them to see that we did not leave that campus without feeling that we had received direction, and suggested that we be given every assistance possible within the scope and limits of their services. (Kendrick, 1963, p. 5)

It cannot be confirmed if this meeting at the University of Missouri was pre-planned or an impromptu stop on the way home. Regardless, the support Dr. Kendrick and Dr. Strahan received from that time forward led to remarkably quick approval of full regional accreditation in the years to come. By December 7, 1956, Evangel's program was endorsed by the University of Missouri – Columbia accreditation committee. This was a significant step towards accreditation by an entity with many political persuasions which may have differed from the philosophy at Evangel. The academic credentials and strength of Dr. Kendrick and Dr. Strahan played a significant role in the accreditation process.

Shortly after this accomplishment, the Department of Education for the State of Missouri itself recognized the teacher certification that had been established at Evangel, and Evangel leaders learned that the North Central Accrediting Association did, in fact, have a study program for institutions who wished to upgrade or improve. Evangel made application to this program and was approved.

In the fourth year of the college a self-study was commenced, [pursuant] to the intention of the college to apply for regional accreditation. This study extended over a three-year period. The outcome of the study as well as the subsequent application can be better told by other persons. It is my personal opinion, however, that it is nothing short of phenomenal the way the college did gain academic prestige and developed an acceptable college program. (Kendrick, 1963, p. 5-6)

Winehouse (1959) includes a brief list of accreditation recognition Evangel received in the founding years in his popular survey of the Assemblies of God:

During its first three years of existence, Evangel College successfully earned the following necessary recognition of its program:

1. Accreditation by the Committee on Accredited Schools and Junior Colleges of the University of Missouri.
2. Approval by the Veterans Administration for training of veterans under the various public laws.
3. Approval of the U.S. Department of Justice, Immigration Service, for the training of non-quota foreign students.
4. Approval of the U.S. Office of Education for listing in Part III of the Directory of Higher Education as an accredited academic college.
5. Approval of the Missouri State Department of Education for teacher certification privileges.

'Evangel College,' Klaude Kendrick, Dean of the School has said, 'was a gift from God.' And in fact it was-with a little assistance from Uncle Sam. (Winehouse, 1959, p. 175)

The rest of the accreditation story will continue when President Ashcroft takes the lead role for Evangel.

While finances and accreditation were clearly a major concern from the beginning, there were many other positive developments in those formative early years that must be mentioned. For example, it was during Dr. Kendrick's tenure that the beloved TRUTH seal was developed. Dr. Kendrick called for the assistance of Dr. Ashcroft, as he often did in those days, to develop a seal for the college. Dr. Ashcroft collaborated with Lloyd Colbaugh, and the TRUTH seal was established, patterned after the VERITAS seal from Harvard but with the added components of a Bible and Cross (Ashcroft, 1988).

Figure 3

The original TRUTH seal

Additionally, just a few months after classes began at Evangel, a prestigious award was created by the faculty to honor those outstanding individuals who contributed to the founding and operation of Evangel ([Faculty Meeting Minutes], 1955). With Dr. Strahan as chair of the committee, the Order of the Shield was established, and Rev. Ralph Riggs was approved as the first honoree. According to a review of faculty minutes from the first 25 years of the institution, the Order of the Shield was changed to the Order of the Golden Shield the following year (1956), and consistently awarded until 1980. At that time, the faculty

Pioneering Spirit

decided to remove the requirement to award it annually and only award it when an outstanding individual was recommended. A list of all known recipients of the Order of the Golden Shield is below:

    1956 – Rev. Ralph M. Riggs

    1957 – E. S. Christoffersen

    1958 – Guy Basye

    1959 – Richard Strahan

    1960 – Andrew Nelli

    1961 – Klaude Kendrick

    1962 – Rev. Charles W. H. Scott

    1963 – Al J. Rediger

    1964 – Rev. Thomas F. Zimmerman and Oscar Love

    1965 – Mrs. Charles W. H. Scott and Henry Krause

    1966 – Guy Braselton and Rev. James Hamill

    1967 – Norm Sommers and Rev. E. M. Clark

    1968 – Wilmoth Price and Harold Gray

    1969 – M. J. Groves and Bernard Bresson

    1970 – Jacob Hershman and Rev. Ivar Frick

    1971 – Walter Block and Mrs. Elsie Isensee

    1972 – Doyle Burgess and Rev. T. E. Gannon

1973 – N. J. Tavani and Angelo Ferri

1974 – Mrs. Walter Block, Sr. (Hattie) and Rev. Arthur H. Parsons

1975 – Rev. J. R. Ashcroft and Mrs. Chuck Wetter (Betty)

1976 – Mrs. Bill Hanawalt (Barbara) and Rev. Ward Williams

1977 – Dr. Rufus Medlin and Rev. G. Raymond Carlson

1978 – Rev. Richard W. Dortch and Max Ephraim

1979 – Rev. Raymond H. Hudson and Russell Umphenour

1980 – Rev. David W. Flower and Edward Hanks

Unrelated to this award, in the same meeting, another interesting item was moved and passed which indicates a sign of the times and how things have changed since the founding of the institution. Faculty decided that for any scheduled test that was taken late, students would have to pay a $1.00 late fee.

Just a few weeks later, in another faculty meeting, Dr. Strahan moved to create an "ex-student association for Evangel College which would include all graduates and former students of the college" ([Faculty Meeting Minutes], 1956, p. 1). This was the birth of what would become the alumni association, and it began before the first year of existence was completed. Dr. Kendrick and Dr. Strahan had many challenges in the first several years, but faculty minutes and other documentation reveal how they kept a keen eye on the items that would contribute to the longevity of the institution most.

One of those items was the consistent focus on the proper development of the students. On April 1, 1958, at 7:30 p.m. a special faculty meeting in the chapel was called. Twenty-two of the twenty-eight faculty members employed at the time attended the meeting. With only a couple months left in his tenure as academic dean and ultimately his involvement with Evangel, Dean Strahan began the meeting and shared that the purpose was to discuss the spiritual problems, attitudes, and conduct of the students related to their spiritual development ([Faculty Meeting Minutes], 1958). The concerns addressed by the dean involved what could be done to encourage a spirit of thankfulness among the students as opposed to having a fault-finding spirit. The dean relayed "...when students start to go downhill spiritually...they also go downhill academically" ([Faculty Meeting Minutes], 1958, p. 1). Ultimately, the meeting was intended to address how to overcome spiritual indifference amongst the students and create an atmosphere for total Christian fellowship.

The conversation was robust, and the hearts the faculty had for the students were on full display. They discussed the development that occurs naturally on a college campus. They discussed how the development at Evangel was different and should be different with the added component of spiritual development. They talked about the loyalty the students had for each other and the dependence they shared while also striving for independence from each other and from their parents. They asked when does a student stop adopting his or her parents' beliefs, and how do they get the students to understand their faith walk was not just a crisis experience, but it was a lifetime journey. At long last, Mr. Clifford Hanks, assistant professor of English, displayed the spiritual leadership that was so evident amongst Dr. Kendrick, Dean Strahan, and the rest of the faculty who were present when he shared the following:

> When I came to this institution, I found a little different feeling about things than I had found elsewhere. I believe our responsibilities to these youngsters goes far beyond the subject matter studied. We should do far more for our students than just teach them our subject matter. We should with some aggressiveness help the student find some stability in life. I feel that we have had a kind of timidity that we are afraid to break. I would like to see a more aggressive approach to solving spiritual problems in an organized way. ([Faculty Meeting Minutes], 1958, p. 2).

And so it was, in the waning hours of Dr. Kendrick's tenure as the founding president, the ethos of Evangel, established and lived out by the faculty he had found and hired across all disciplines, was on full display as a model for the hundreds of faculty members who would follow.

Resignation

On February 11 – 14, 1958, the General Presbytery spent considerable time discussing a proposal to consolidate the administrative positions of Evangel College and Central Bible Institute ([Important Dates}, n.d.). This proposal was put forth in a letter submitted to the General Presbytery from General Superintendent Ralph Riggs. In the meeting, after discussion and consideration of the proposal, a Bro. Bush made a motion to proceed to implement the plan, and it was seconded and passed. This was the first documented attempt at consolidation between the two flagship schools, one a Bible school and one a liberal arts school, located just a few miles from the headquarters for the AG denomination in Springfield, Missouri.

According to archived oral history interviews, there are multiple reasons for this attempt at consolidation, not the least of which was a pending financial crisis. Dr. Ward Williams was the academic dean who would succeed Dr. Kendrick in 1960 and complete the accreditation effort. His expertise and career consisted of assisting multiple AG colleges with accreditation issues in different ways. According to his analysis, the first two years of operation at Evangel were financially reasonable because the Freshmen and Sophomore years typically consists of general classes offered en masse.

> When they got to the junior year – that's when you have to offer these specialized courses, all of a sudden you have many more faculty members, you have small classes – they went in debt so fast that by February they were $450,000 in the hole. (Williams, 1988, p. 7).

Williams goes on to indicate that this was the direct reason Riggs was not reelected in the subsequent General Council election for superintendent. It should also be noted that Dr. Ashcroft indicates that the deficit was closer to $300,000 (Ashcroft, 1988). Regardless, in dollars adjusted for 1955, the debt seemed insurmountable.

This might explain the financial implications of the first presidential transition, but Dr. Kendrick shared a decision he and Dr. Strahan made that showed an incredible amount of self-sacrificial leadership to address the financial challenges in the best way they could. Perhaps the rationale for the first presidential resignation could be best explained in Dr. Kendrick's own words:

Another matter [in addition to accreditation] that gave special concern to Dr. Strahan and me was the relationship between Evangel College and Central Bible Institute... As this matter was given attention, we also came to the conclusion that there was much needless duplication in the two programs...As this concept grew, it became such a conviction with us that we finally proposed to the Education Department as well as members of the administration of Central Bible Institute to work and look towards some type of amalgamation...As a consequence of our feeling, both Dr. Strahan and I resigned so that the administrative structure of Evangel College could be in a position to adjust to whatever new type administration might be approved. ([Notes from Klaude Kendrick], 1988, p. 6)

In addition to the financial improvements which were assumed could result from this amalgamation, Dr. Ashcroft also considered the opportunity it could bring to step toward university status (Ashcroft, 1988). In combining a strong theology program, that could develop into a seminary, with a growing liberal arts program, there was thought that this combination of the schools could produce a university system. As time would tell, this dream did not materialize, and the economies that were pursued did not last either. Dr. Kendrick states, "It was always a matter of personal regret to me that the structure was not carried further so that long-range economies might be realized" ([Notes from Klaude Kendrick, 1988, p. 6). He goes on to share that a full consolidation would be needed for the needless duplication to be corrected.

Subsequently, Dr. Strahan and his family returned home to Texas to serve at the University of Houston and plant Calvary Church in Houston. Dr. Kendrick remained at Evangel and served as the academic dean to continue the work toward accreditation. He then was asked to serve as the president of Southwestern Bible College in 1960. Dr. Ward Williams succeeded him as the dean, and he stated the following:

> This school owes an enormous debt to Strahan…He came up here with the determination that this school could be absolutely first class in every regard…Everything was done right…I didn't have to undo one single thing that Strahan did. He laid the foundations here absolutely soundly educationally…This is the only school we've had that was started by people who started it right, and it's continued this way to this day. Other schools have had to become professional over a period of years. (Williams, 1988, p. 13-14)

When discussing Dr. Kendrick, many alumni from those first three years characterized him as a fellow "Pioneer." He was one who was a successful academician who was skilled at starting programs. As the first attempt at consolidation began, the presidency gave way to a man familiar with Evangel from before it began. He had actually been in discussions with Ralph Riggs ten years before it started. Dr. Kendrick was born on June 5, 1917, and passed away on August 28, 2010.

Dr. J. Robert Ashcroft Presidency (1959 – 1974)

Dr. J. (James) Robert Ashcroft was born on December 18, 1911, in Philadelphia, Pennsylvania. He received his B.S. degree from Connecticut State Teachers College followed by an M.A. in Education from New York University. He did further work toward a doctorate at NYU before entering vocational ministry. He was ordained as a minister in the Assemblies of God in 1932. He traveled as an evangelist from 1929 to 1932. He also pastored in Chicago and then in Hartford, Connecticut from 1931 to 1947. While pastoring in Chicago, he also taught part-time at the Great Lakes Bible Institute from 1939 to 1941.

A letter dated February 6, 1945, reveals an introductory correspondence between Ralph Riggs and J. Robert Ashcroft. Ashcroft is delivering a response to a form letter sent by Riggs where he had requested recommendations for potential faculty members for an AG liberal arts college. This followed a recommendation from the Educational Committee he chaired as Assistant Superintendent, a position to which he was elected in 1943. The General Presbytery voted in favor of the recommendation, but the 1945 General Council put the plans on hold. Ashcroft revealed an openness and support for this type of program in his response when he stated,

> An L.A. [liberal arts] College would have meant much when I was at that age. The most important thing about it would have been what it symbolizes...Our movement should have a school as a symbol of our thinking about the Power of God working through well trained personnel. (Ashcroft, 1945, p. 1)

He went on to share his feelings that this type of college for the AG was an immediate necessity to serve the veterans who were returning from World War 2.

Perhaps this interaction, and Ashcroft's clear support of such a program, was the impetus for his becoming the head of the Christian Education Department at Central Bible Institute in 1947. By 1953, he became the National Secretary for Education for the Assemblies of God until 1958, when he became the second president of Evangel College. He served as president of both Evangel and Central Bible Institute until 1963 when he became the full-time president of Evangel. He remained Evangel's president until 1974. After Evangel, he spent time pastoring in Brussels, Belgium before becoming president of Valley Forge Christian College from 1982 to 1984 and then president of Berean University (now Global University) from 1985 to 1989.

Throughout his career, he authored many articles related to higher education, Christian faith, and Pentecostalism along with two books, *Ways of Understanding God's Word* and *Sequence of the Supernatural*. He was also well known for his poetry. He married Grace P. Larson in 1935, and they had three sons: Robert, John, and Wesley. Following Grace's death, he married Mabel in 1987.

During his tenure as president of Evangel, eight major buildings were constructed and accreditation was granted by the North Central Association of Colleges and Schools, the National Council for Accreditation of Teacher Education, and the National Association of Schools of Music. He also received an honorary doctorate from Southern California College (now Vanguard University).

A review of his correspondence shows an incredible breadth of connection and recognition with leaders across the Christian faith and around the world. Such correspondence includes personal letters from spiritual leaders like Oral Roberts to influential figures of national politics like Ronald Reagan. His correspondence also revealed a depth of character and care for the individuals with whom he interacted. From thank you notes and notes of congratulations to fellow presidents to notes of encouragement to alumni and friends, his writing ability seemed to be endless in a time before computers made mass messages so simple. It is no wonder he was revered on campus and beyond as a spiritual giant and father or grandfather figure to so many. His humble spirit and endearing nature along with his connection to Evangel from before it began made him an obvious choice to become the second president in the young institution's history.

Inauguration

On September 4, 1958, Dr. J. Robert Ashcroft was inaugurated as the president of Evangel College and Central Bible Institute ([Inauguration Program], 1958). The inaugural address was delivered by Dr. C. Hoyt Watson, President of Seattle Pacific College, and the presidential charge was given by Ralph Riggs himself. The deep, personal friendship Riggs and Ashcroft shared was obvious. In his charge, Riggs states, "We assure you, my good brother, that you have the loyalty, love and support of the officers, faculties, students, and constituency of the Assemblies of God, as well as of our kind friends and neighbors" (Riggs, 1958, p. 3).

Ashcroft's response to the charge was brief, but in it he pledges allegiance to God, the Church, the flag of the United States, and both Evangel and CBI. A few days before his official inauguration, Ashcroft delivered his first address to the joint opening session of the Advisory Council and Faculties of Evangel and CBI, and he delivered it again to a joint meeting of students of both institutions as well. In it, he laid the groundwork for how he planned to lead and the goals of his administration. He used the story of Moses' training in the Old Testament as the backdrop for his comments (Ashcroft, 1958). He made the case that Moses grew up with a liberal arts education in all the wisdom Egypt had to offer combined with the Christian education and training provided by his mother who reared him as his nurse. This is the type of education and environment Ashcroft believed existed at Evangel. He shared how Evangel was bucking the trend of the direction culture was headed. Quoting a letter that had been sent to the headquarters of the denomination decrying the stampede away from responsibility the country was seeing, he said, "We must get our people into the battle, but first we must get some battle into our people" (Ashcroft, 1958, p. 2).

The feeling of providing an educational experience in a total learning environment that went against the grain of culture has existed since the formation of Evangel. At another point in his inauguration speech, Ashcroft said, "I share this with you because I want you to know that the program at Evangel College is going to be at right angles to the program in society today" (Ashcroft, 1958, p. 2). To sum up his foundational beliefs about the importance of the mission of Evangel, he said, "Christian young people are in moral danger, and Christian education is the last stand against moral degeneracy" (Ashcroft, 1958, p.3).

Finally, Ashcroft speaks about the four emphases of his administration as president of Evangel and CBI:

> As I lay before the Lord in the early parts of this year, I felt the Lord spoke to me about the four great emphases of my administration of Evangel College and Central Bible Institute. And here they are: First, character development; secondly, increase of knowledge of the content courses; thirdly, a development of the ability to write well, and lastly, developing the ability to speak well. (Ashcroft, 1958, p. 4)

His final admonition to the first group of students under his leadership as president was this:

Don't ever lose it. Don't let any professor, any friend, or any literature ever put in your brain the idea that you're not going to accomplish anything in this world. Keep it ever ablaze in your heart. You are going to set the world on fire! (Ashcroft, 1958, p.7)

Operations of the College

While Dr. Ashcroft was education secretary for the AG, before he became president of Evangel, he conducted a national survey of AG youth to assist in the development of the curricular offerings of the young institution. His report captured the interests and attitudes of students interested in a school like Evangel. With 187 responses to the survey, it was certainly not comprehensive. However, it did illuminate some important pieces of information that would assist Evangel, and ultimately Dr. Ashcroft, in its continued growth.

According to Ashcroft's survey, the top locales where respondents were from included Kansas City, KS, Inglewood, CA, Fort Worth, TX, Oklahoma City, OK, and North Little Rock, AR ([Education Department Survey], 1957). The responses were nearly evenly split with 91 boys and 96 girls. In terms of study areas of interest, the top three were overwhelmingly the majority and included Business, Undecided, and Engineering ([Education Department Survey], 1957). These areas were followed by Skilled Labor, The Ministry, Teaching, and Nursing. A similar survey put out by the Campus Ambassador office yielded more responses with similar results. The main difference between the surveys was that the Campus Ambassador survey was sent to students who were already enrolled as undergraduates in college. That survey indicated the top three areas of interest for students in what they were already studying were Education, Business, and Engineering. All of this information helped shape the focus and efforts Dr. Ashcroft had as he took office.

In March of 1958, a little more than a year before the first graduation ceremony would take place, efforts began to assist students to find employment or graduate school placement. A report to the board of administration included five pages for recommended placement services ([Recommended Placement Services], 1958). The report recommended the formation of a placement office that would accomplish three tasks. The placement office would take responsibility for helping students find part-time work to facilitate their ability to afford their schooling, help them find placement upon graduation, and conduct follow-up activities to study the success of the graduates while providing continued guidance to those who have been out of college for several years ([Recommended Placement Services], 1958). This recommendation was directly related to information provided by the North Central Association as a service that was provided by accredited institutions. With the continued focus on accreditation, the report was accepted in full by the board administration with one amendment that students be required to pay a service fee of $5.00 to utilize the placement office. This was done to assist in funding the launch of this new office.

In the midst of all the administrative, financial, and curriculum challenges and developments that were taking place, it might be easy to forget the important work that persisted in the classroom. This young institution successfully navigated a freshmen, sophomore, and junior year only to arrive at its fourth year of existence and the impending senior year culminating in the first commencement in its history. In his analysis, Burtchaell (1998) reveals most schools struggle through the first several years before eventually making it to a graduation event. At Evangel, it occurred in the traditional fourth year for the students who came in as Freshmen.

There were 37 individuals who would go down in history as the very first graduating class in the history of Evangel. These individuals were:

1959 Graduates

BACHELOR OF ARTS

Downey, Edmund L..	Nolan, Jean Etta Hamilton
Hamilton, Joan Ella	Stinchcomb, Elizabeth
Hoge, Thomasine Lois	Watrous, Joanne Carol
Jackway, Leo Kenneth	Zimmerman, Thomas F.

BACHELOR OF SCIENCE

Baker, Edith Lavon	Ernst, Elizabeth
Cargnel, Jacqueline Ann	Foote, Freida Lillian
Cathcart, Lavera May	Hanson, Ronald Duane
Cornwell, Sharon Ruth	Hosier, Phyllis

Pioneering Spirit

Cottrell, Shirley Ann	Johnson, Ruth
Davis, John W.	Keller, Phillip B.
Downey, Hester A.	Malone, Esther
Erickson, Wanda Louise	Nimmo, DelWayne

BACHELOR OF MUSIC

Davis, James Eugene

BACHELOR OF BUSINESS ADMINISTRATION

Allen, Marvin Everett	Martin, Janell
Beeman, Clarence Donald	Powers, Jack
Casebeer, Robert Adrian	Reis, Caroline
Chancellor, Don	Roe, Robert David
Gardner, Gary Norman	

ASSOCIATE IN BUSINESS (2 YEAR)

Barkley, Loretta Mae	Spence, Shirley Ann
Bell, Joann	

While the first graduation in Evangel's existence occurred, the school was also navigating its first attempt at consolidation with CBI. This attempt was never able to get past the combining of the administrative levels of the schools, which only included the president, business manager, and promotional efforts (Williams, 1988). After just one year, during the year of Evangel's first graduation (58-59), CBI requested to have its own promotional department (Williams, 1988). Grant Wacker, who had served as the promotions director for both schools, came to Evangel, and CBI was granted autonomy for their own promotions. After the second year (59-60), Dr. Kendrick, who had served as the academic dean, was named president of Southwestern Bible College, and Dr. Ward Williams became the dean at Evangel. During his first three years, Dr. Ashcroft's main office was at CBI (Williams, 1988). This gave Dr. Williams quite a bit of liberty at Evangel to work toward accreditation. "I was given a very free hand during that time in policy and finances and so on. My major contribution to this school, of course, is in the area of accreditation" (Williams, 1988, p. 8).

After Williams' third year in the role of academic dean (62-63), he shares the story of how the consolidation came to an end:

> At the end of three more years, at the end of my third year, CBC decided they wanted to have their own president and their own business manager. They wanted to pull out of this dual arrangement. They expected Ashcroft to stay there. The biggest surprise was that Ashcroft stayed with Evangel, which CBC had not anticipated. He cast his lot here. Previous to the dual arrangement Brother Peterson had been the president of CBC. I'm not going to put it on tape, now, Betty, but there are things there that involve the

relationship of Brown and Peterson and Evans that are a story of their own, which we'll not get into here. (Williams, 1988, p. 8).

Williams also believed the different philosophies of the schools contributed to discontinuing the consolidation. CBI was a direct responsibility of the Executive Presbytery since that group also served as the Board of Directors while Evangel had a separate Board of Directors that served as a buffer between being directly supervised by the General Council (Williams, 1988). He predicted that eventually, due to financial duress, the two schools would have to merge completely, and he believed Evangel would be the lead school when that occurred (Williams, 1988). According to Williams, CBI's simpler curriculum allowed for larger classes, and thus more stable financial issues while Evangel was still running deficits though enrollment was growing. He believed this was due to the accounting that was merged at that time. "This again is partly accounting, Betty. The thing I fought and did not win was that no operational money shall be spent for equipment…Now what they've done is, they've taken an operating budget and dropped capital investment in it, and that's not right" (Williams, 1988, p. 29). Eventually, this would become a very detrimental issue for Dr. Ashcroft and his administration.

The end of the consolidation was announced to the national constituency of the AG through *The Pentecostal Evangel* with an explanation and rationale behind the decision to separate the presidency (Presidency, 1963). In that article, the decision was stated as being made by the Evangel Board of Directors and approved and supported by the Executive Presbytery (Presidency, 1963). It is also mentioned that Thomas Zimmerman, superintendent of the General Council at that time, "declared that the growth of CBI and Evangel makes it imperative that each should have its own president" (Presidency, 1968, p. 28). In addition to exceptional growth being mentioned as the main reason for the separation, Zimmerman also pointed out that Evangel's first permanent building was nearly completed, and students were responding enthusiastically to a new program developing vocational volunteers known as SCOPE (Service Corps of Pentecostal Endeavor) (Presidency, 1963). SCOPE was a precursor to what is known today as Crosswalk Student Ministries, which is where opportunities for volunteer service and ministry are developed and provided for Evangel students. It was made known that CBI desired for President Ashcroft to remain as CBI's president, but the Executive Presbytery felt otherwise.

Just as the presidencies were separated, and Dr. Ashcroft assumed the full-time presidential position at Evangel, the first permanent building was being completed. In fact, Ashcroft's tenure as president saw several building projects completed with seven which still remain in use on campus as of this writing. The years listed indicate the year the building was opened. Planning, fundraising, and development activities for many of the buildings were in process for many years in advance of the years listed.

> 1963 – KLAUDE KENDRICK LIBRARY: The first permanent structure built on the EU campus, it is named for Dr. Klaude Kendrick, Evangel's first president (1955-1958). It houses the Betty Chase Archives. Betty began working on the Evangel project in 1953, served several communication positions through 1987, and served as archivist until she retired in 2007.

1967 – J. ROBERT ASHCROFT ACTIVITIES CENTER: The gymnasium was named for Dr. J. Robert Ashcroft, second president of EU (1958-1974). The facility's unique architectural peaks reach 43 feet. It contains offices for the intercollegiate Athletic Department.

1968 – SPENCE HALL: Named for Inez Spence, a supervisor of both men's and women's residences (1956-1966), this building was opened as the first permanent women's residence hall. Spence Hall can house 216 students.

1969 – PERKIN APARTMENTS: Named for The Rev. Noel Perkin, director of Assemblies of God Foreign Missions for 33 years (1927-1959), the apartments are designated for married students. Each of the 16 units has 650 square feet of floor space.

1970 – KRAUSE HALL: This three-story male residence hall can house 216 students. It was named for inventor Henry Krause, member of the first Board of Directors and what was then known as the Evangel College Council.

1970 – WALTHER HALL: This residence hall was named for Grace Walther, the first Director of Student Life and organizer of Evangel's student teaching program (1955-1977). Walther Hall can house 216 students.

1972 – SCOTT HALL: Named for the Rev. Charles W.H. and Gertrude Scott; he was the first chairman of Evangel's Board of Directors, and she helped to found the Evangel College Ladies Auxiliary. Scott Hall can house 216 students. (Logsdon, 2018, p. 2).

As more permanent buildings became a part of the growing campus, it allowed for growth in extracurricular activities such as athletics as well. It is a commonly accepted notion that athletics can be considered the front porch of a college or university. The meaning behind this phrase is that athletics, if administered and marketed correctly, can serve as an attraction and recruiting system for a broad cross-section of students, athletes and non-athlete alike. A full review of Evangel's history of sports for the first 25 years is listed in Appendix G. Men's basketball has been a part of the Evangel experience from the very first year. No other sport was added until Ashcroft became president.

During Ashcroft's presidency, the following sports began: Men's Track (59-60), Men's Tennis (59-60), Baseball (64-65), Men's Golf (65-66), Women's Tennis (65-66), Women's Volleyball (66-67), Women's Track (66-67), Softball (66-67), Wrestling (67-68), Men's Soccer (68-69), Field Hockey (68-69, only year offered), Cross Country (69-70). Interestingly, towards the end of Ashcroft's tenure was when the Education Amendments of 1972 were passed that included Title IX. Title IX prohibited sex-based discrimination in any school or any other education program which received funding from the federal government (*Title IX and Sex Discrimination*, 2021). This included schools offering federal financial aid. Title IX had been in discussion and had several different precursors stemming from the Civil Rights Act of 1964. This might explain, in part, the context behind the decisions to begin several female-specific sports during that time.

It should also be noted that several sports were removed during or immediately after Ashcroft's tenure as well. Those sports include: Softball (70-71, though it would return later and is still offered as of this writing), Wrestling (72-73), Women's Track (72-73, this sport would return and is still active), Men's Soccer (73-74, this sport started back up in 2015), Men's Track (74-75, this sport would also return and is still active), Men's Golf (74-75,

Pioneering Spirit

this sport would also return and is still active), Cross Country (75-76, this sport would also return and is still active).

While athletics can certainly be a strategy to increase enrollment, there are many other factors that can contribute to positive enrollment growth. Accreditation is another aspect many leaders thought would help stabilize enrollment at the time. The enrollment trends show a slow and steady increase in enrollment during most of Ashcroft's presidency with no significant bump after 1965, when accreditation was achieved.

Figure 4

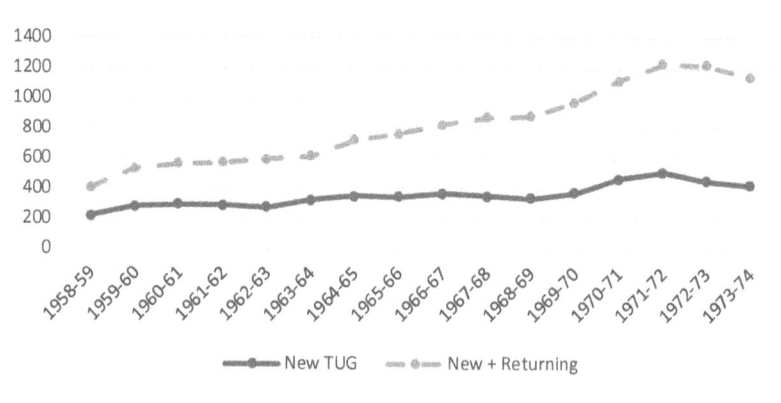

Ashcroft Presidency Enrollment Trend

Regardless, it is quite remarkable to consider that enrollment tripled under Ashcroft's leadership.

Another strategy to expand offerings and potentially recruit more students might be to offer summer school. According to archived faculty minutes, on February 25, 1960, the Board of Directors voted to authorize the offering of courses during the summer. However, there is no summer enrollment recorded in the annual registrar's report until the 67-68 school year. The gears of higher education grind slowly.

Related to enrollment, it is important to note the change in tuition. In Ashcroft's first year, tuition at Evangel was $12.00 per credit hour. In his final year, it was $35.00.

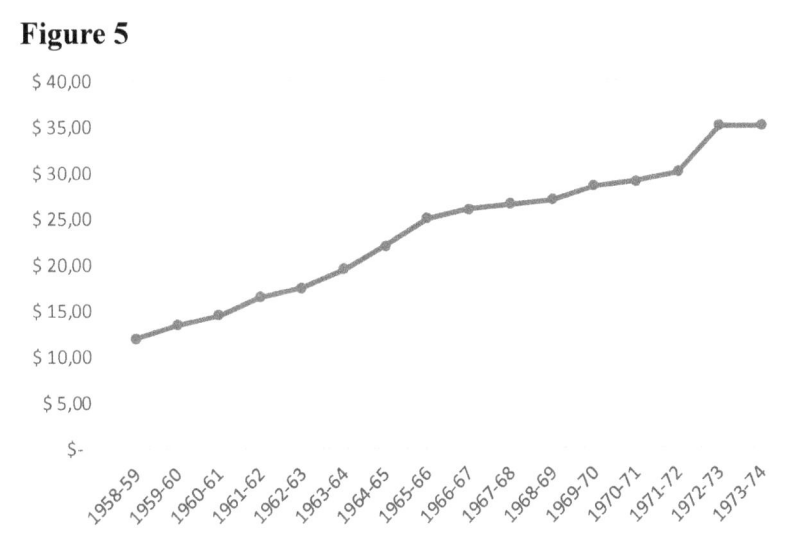

Figure 5

Ashcroft Presidency - Tuition Per Hour Cost Trend

There are many variables to consider when reviewing the budget and finances for a higher education institution, especially a private institution like Evangel which leans so heavily on tuition and fundraising efforts. Many presidents are considered the top fundraiser for the institution. An emphasis on fundraising activities has increased in recent years, but it is still helpful to consider the fundraising efforts over the years.

One interesting idea that came from the leadership at Evangel in 1974 was to create an Assemblies of God Foundation for Higher Education. The purpose was to make funds available immediately, and it was suggested that it be governed by a board completely separated from any vested interest in any of the schools. It was believed that the foundation could be capitalized with $1,000,000 at once, and the money could be secured with bonds issued at a modest rate of 6%. A foundation arm of the denomination's leading financial services company still exists as of this writing. In addition to this unique fundraising mechanism, more traditional fundraising practices were in effect from the beginning.

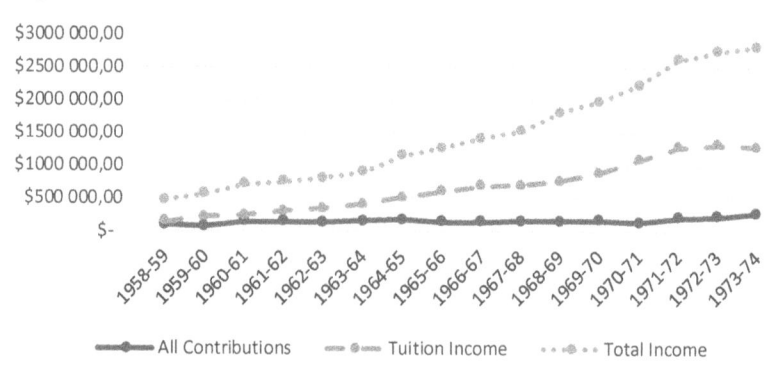

Figure 6

Ashcroft Presidency - Contributions, Enrollment Income, Total Income

Seeing all these data points together can provide a picture of data that helps tell part of the story of Ashcroft's tenure.

One of the most important events that occurred during Ashcroft's time was that Evangel achieved regional accreditation. To achieve this within ten years of being founded is a remarkable feat that reveals a depth of academic acumen uncommon in such young institutions. It also reveals several divine coincidences at key points in the process. Kendrick revealed from the beginning he believed every instruction he received was to pursue accreditation (Kendrick, n.d.).

He continued that pursuit when he became academic dean and was able to begin a self-study with the North Central

Accrediting Association just four years into the new institution's existence. With a self-study period of three years, the first self-study was completed and submitted for review in 1962. Dr. Ward Williams continued the effort begun by Dr. Kendrick when he became dean while Ashcroft was president.

It was clear that Evangel had the attention, and ultimately the support, of the accrediting agency. Assistant Secretary Richard H. Davis (1962) wrote a letter responding to the submission of the self-study with clear care, encouragement, and support. In it he wrote, "Although the Board voted to accept Evangel College's self-study report, it decided not to authorize an examination of Evangel College this year" (Davis, 1962, p. 1). He went on to share how this was an intentional step taken by the board to protect Evangel from the possibility of an unsatisfactory accrediting examination. Should Evangel receive an unsatisfactory examination, it would result in the requirement to wait for three years before reapplying. He then stated, "However, if any applying institution is temporarily delayed in the self-study phase of the accreditation process, our experience has shown that this is often the fastest course to regional accreditation" (Davis, 1962, p. 1). In his letter he also shares that Evangel's strengths were recognized by the board, but there was concern about inadequate faculty, low salaries, admission standards, library holdings and building, administrative organization of institution, teacher education and student teacher program, and the relationship between the College and Bible Institute. He recommended an accreditation consultant to assist Evangel in overcoming the stated weaknesses. It is interesting that one year later, Evangel and CBI would revert to separate entities with separated administrations. Perhaps the striving for accreditation played a role in ending the first attempt at consolidation.

Just one year after the consolidation ended, another self-study report was submitted to the North Central Accreditation Agency for review in 1964. Totaling nearly 300 pages, this report was accepted and put through the full review process. Much has been written about Evangel's accreditation, but there are several key points which further demonstrate divine coincidences that have peppered Evangel's rich history.

During the accrediting team's visit to the campus, they made several recommendations to position Evangel for accreditation approval. The recommendations involved the library, faculty, laboratories, and equipment, and Evangel met the recommendations. On the subsequent visit to Chicago for the final accreditation review meeting, Dr. Williams and Dr. Ashcroft met with members who had not visited the campus and only worked off the paper application and recommendations of the visiting committee. What concerned the final review committee most was academic freedom.

> We were a Christian college. We were an evangelical college. We were, of all the horrible things, a Pentecostal college, and how in the world could people as narrow as that have academic freedom? And that's about all they talked to us about for an hour and a half, the matter of academic freedom. (Williams, 1988, p. 10).

There are several stories Williams then relays which are coincidental in nature and deserve to be shared in full.

> Finally, as a kind of test question and example of what he was driving at, one of the committee members asked President

Ashcroft, 'Mr. President, what would you do if one of your English teachers wanted to teach a course in Joyce'--the author of Ulysses, of course, and other books. I don't think Ashcroft was aware of this, but I was able to say, 'Bob, let me answer that question.' and I said, And I spoke to the man 'Sir, it pleases me to tell you that the chairman of English Department is Mrs. Elsie Elmendorf. She is pursuing her doctorate at the University of Missouri, and the subject of her doctoral thesis is The Christ Image in Joyce. And, Betty. I can't tell you how much I was aware that God arranged the one to be asked. God put that thing in our hands. That cleared the discussion. We talked a few more minutes, and they said that if the school was broadminded enough to allow the head of the English Department to write a thesis on The Christ Image in Joyce, we were broadminded enough to meet their requirements. Then they let us go. (Williams, 1988, p. 10)

Williams would go on to explain how Mrs. Elmendorf could have chosen a number of literary authors to study and just so happened to choose Joyce. She also never completed her doctorate, but her selected thesis served an important purpose that was a major factor in satisfying the concerns around academic freedom.

Another illustration involved Dr. Williams' efforts to increase the academic strength of the faculty Evangel was utilizing. He allowed for extended sabbaticals to keep faculty with Ph.Ds. as he worked towards accreditation. He also encouraged those pursuing different degrees to consider programs that would be most helpful to the accreditation efforts. Dr. Alexander Karmarkovic was a pastor in Moorhead, Minnesota. He had gotten a degree in History, and Dr. Williams encouraged him to consider an advanced degree in political science. In his view, there were already enough History majors and teachers, but he did not know of any political scientists in the AG. Dr. Karmarkovic agreed to switch to Political Science, and Dr. Williams was able to get a pass on the Great Northern Railroad so Dr. Karmarkovic could receive his doctorate 350 miles away at the University of Minnesota. He rode that train for two years while completing his degree.

Once completed, he was one of the final faculty members with a Ph. D who helped Evangel meet the accreditation standards, and he went on to lead the political science area at Evangel for many years. The importance in this story lies in the small detail of how Dr. Williams was able to get a free pass on the railroad to facilitate Dr. Karmarkovic getting this important degree.

When Williams was asked how he was able to procure a free pass on the Great Northern Railroad, he shared the following story:

> That's due to the superstitious nature of J. J. Hill. J. J. Hill and his partner built the first railroad between Minneapolis and St. Paul, and his partner faced a divorce by his wife. So his wife couldn't take the railroad away from him he sold his half to J. J. Hill for a dollar, and Hill never gave it back. On the basis of owning that little short railroad, J. J. Hill built the Great Northern Railroad out to North Dakota and clear to the West Coast. This is not the place to tell stories about the Great Northern Railroad, but it has been the railroad that served me when I lived in North Dakota. I have talked to the people that knew J. J. Hill personally when he was riding fat ponies out there and driving stakes in the prairie as to where his railroad should run. But he was a Catholic, and he was superstitious. He wanted to give free passes to all the nuns and the priests, and you can't do that unless you give them

to Protestants as well. He's long since dead, but the Great Northern Railroad had a very generous policy, which other railroads didn't have, of passes for clergy. And I knew this, and I had had a Great Northern pass at one time, and so I got a pass for him on that basis. It was just a Great Northern policy I knew about. (Williams, 1988, p. 13).

As Dr. Williams drew near to finally gaining accreditation for Evangel, the stress of the process gave him asthma, which he dealt with for the rest of his life. All of this built up to an exciting announcement that would validate all the work Kendrick and Ashcroft had led since the beginning of the institution. On March 31, 1965, official word was received that Evangel College had been approved and admitted as a member of the North Central Association of Colleges and Secondary Schools. Accreditation had been achieved, and shortly afterward, Dr. Williams stepped down as dean to return to the faculty.

Resignation

Throughout his tenure as president, Dr. Ashcroft was focused on treating every person with whom he connected with grace and dignity. It was a part of his philosophical belief to treat every student as an individual and with an extra portion of dignity and love. This was also the case in the way he communicated with faculty, staff, and individuals outside of Evangel.

Because of this deep conviction, it is no surprise to see this attitude persist in his communication with the leadership of the Assemblies of God through the process of his resignation. Here again, finances played an integral role in this presidential transition. According to Williams, it had to do with bookkeeping (Williams, 1988). He indicated there should be a procedural difference between how the accounting was done for capital expenditures compared to how it should have been done. While discussing it, he said, "…I think that President Ashcroft had to take the blame for deficits that did not exist" (Williams, 1988, p. 29). When asked whether it was the Evangel Board of Directors or the Executive Presbytery for the AG who wanted a certain type of bookkeeping, he responded laughingly, "I'd be wiser not to answer that question, probably" (Williams, 1988, p. 30).

In any event, a brief synopsis of the dates and communication leading up to Ashcroft's resignation can provide helpful context. During this time in the school's history, the fiscal year ran from July 1 to June 30.

March 8, 1973 – In a faculty meeting, Dr. Ashcroft states that it is expected for Evangel to finish the fiscal year in the black and will have a budget enrollment or better next year ([Faculty Meeting Minutes], 1973, March 8).

April 12, 1973 – "President Ashcroft reported that the Committee on Administrative Structure, composed of the Executive Committee of the Board of Directors minus the President, had a special meeting in Atlanta on April 5 with the President serving as a resource person. He has been asked to recommend ways in which the administrative officers could have a more direct line of accountability and could also be reduced in number without any loss of personnel and without salary reductions. These recommendations are to be presented to the Board of Directors at their May meeting. The President solicited the prayers and counsel of the faculty for these decisions" ([Faculty Meeting Minutes], 1973, April 12, p. 1)

In the same meeting, Dr. Ashcroft shared concerns with the upcoming budget for the 73-74 school and fiscal year. Due to inflation and enrollment trends, it was estimated that the school would need to cut $160,000 from the budget. Additionally, the fuel crisis was estimated to cost $150,000 in capital outlay for stokers and storage tanks. Dr. Ashcroft reminded that faculty "...that it is not God's will to 'cut back' and that we need not be defeated by such problems as finances and enrollment if we maintain a Spirit-filled college" ([Faculty Meeting Minutes], 1973, April 12, p. 1).

August 1, 1973 – Ashcroft sends a letter where he shares two deep concerns with the Executive Presbytery for the AG. First, he shares that the reorganization of the administration, which most likely came as a result from the meeting in Atlanta earlier in the spring, was related to three of the administrators of the school resigning. All at once, Dr. Robert Cooley, Dean of the College, Dr. William McTeer, former Business Manager and current Dean of Faculty, and Dr. C. Barker Harrison, Director of Records and Registration, all resigned due to the change in the administration reorganization (Ashcroft, 1973). Secondly, and more concerning to Ashcroft at the time, he shared that an error in the budgeting had been found. Just five days before the close of the fiscal year the leadership believed they would be within budget. What they found was a deficit of $125,000 which had not been accounted for properly. In this two-page letter, Ashcroft sums it up with, "The mistake is inexcusable, but explainable. Data was accurate, but projections were inaccurate" (Ashcroft, 1973, p. 1). He reiterates that there was no intent to mislead and asks for support as he promises to rectify the situation.

August 15, 1973 – A few days after his letter to the Executive Presbytery, Dr. Ashcroft sends his annual report to the broader group known as the General Presbytery for the AG. In this letter he is bit more upbeat while still sharing that the deficit was $162,520. He again explains there was no misuse of funds, but that it was an error in the year-end projection based on available data. The expenditures which caused the deficit were from essential fixed cost items like increased utilities, faculty and staff benefits, storm damage, and contracted instruction costs (Ashcroft, 1973, August 15). This was the timeframe when fuel shortages were part of the broader economic outlook which drove energy prices higher. He goes on to share several positive updates related to a record year in fundraising, enrollment trends improving, and a strong spiritual climate on campus. He ends the letter with gratitude for the body of leaders who he believes will support Evangel and walk with him through this trial. He begins and ends his report with a verse from Proverbs 24:10 which he quotes "If thou faint in the day of adversity, thy strength is small."

August 29, 1973 – As the fall semester began, General Superintendent Thomas Zimmerman sent Dr. Ashcroft a letter with the response from the General Presbytery. In it, he conveyed gratitude and support for Evangel and its mission, but shared disappointment with what had occurred. The General Presbytery instructed the Evangel Board of Directors to set up procedures to not permit extra budgetary expenditures without approval from the board's Finance Committee. They implored Evangel to replace the funds at the earliest possible date and that no capital expense will be approved until the budget was back in balance (Zimmerman, 1973). The letter ends by saying, "May we assure you, Brother Ashcroft, that we have detected no lessening of interest on the part of the General Presbytery for Evangel College or its purposes, but there has been a most frustrated feeling because of so many crises growing out of the fiscal administration of the college" (Zimmerman, 1973, p. 2).

September 7, 1973 – Superintendent Zimmerman visited Ashcroft in person after the letter from the General Presbytery was written. Following that meeting, Ashcroft wrote Zimmerman a letter ensuring his understanding of the actions that were expected and adding his own elements which he hoped to show were meeting those expectations. In that letter he stated his gratitude for the continued support by both leadership groups for Evangel, and he identifies with their disappointment. In another strong show of his self-sacrificial leadership, he states, "…I did feel fortunate in being able to face the Presbytery directly and take the consequence myself" (Ashcroft, 1973, September 7, p. 1). He lists his understanding of seven specific instructions which were given followed by 10 procedures he and the administration were implementing to meet those instructions.

November 15, 1973 – A special faculty meeting was called following the regular meeting of the Executive Presbytery. The purpose of the meeting was to report actions that were taken concerning Evangel. In summary, several statements of support were shared with a motion duly adopted by the Executive Presbytery which implored all districts, churches, and individuals who were members of the AG to include Evangel in their ongoing prayers and financial support. A copy of the notes and minutes from this meeting can be found in Appendix H.

December 10, 1973 – At the end of a semester fraught with turmoil and just after agreeing to another five-year term offered by the Board of Directors a year before, Dr. J. Robert Ashcroft submitted his letter of resignation as President. He cuts straight to the point in his opening paragraph by stating, "The events of recent days since our October Board meeting and comments of Board members reported to me lead me to believe that the best interest of the College and its current achievements would be best served by relieving me of the responsibilities of the President's Office" (Ashcroft, 1973, December 10, p. 1). Ashcroft declared that it was a deep conviction with him that this decision was what was best for the college to retain its best personnel, maintain its enrollment and continue its favorable public image. He does allude to his reasoning as being due to rumors which were destroying the administration's ability to secure funding. He mentions rumors that the administration had lost support of the board. He also appeals to the need for a smooth transition to maintain Evangel's highly respected academic and economic standing. With grace, humility, and an unwavering desire to act in the best interest of the institution, Dr. J. Robert Ashcroft's tenure as the second president of Evangel had come to an end. That same evening, he would make the announcement to the faculty and staff at the annual appreciation dinner celebrating the Christmas holiday at the end of the fall semester.

    The next day a press release was sent from the AG national office with a litany of Ashcroft's accomplishments and a commendation for his work from Superintendent Zimmerman. From there, the spring was filled with different groups celebrating and honoring Dr. Ashcroft for the formative job he had accomplished in the development of Evangel. He was given gifts, honored at parties, and publicly celebrated in a variety of ways. Yet, while those events were taking place, he continued to keep his focus on Evangel and finishing well. Once the next president was selected, he shared multiple correspondence with him to establish a smooth transition. He even made sure to send one final, strong fundraising appeal when he noticed a dip in fundraising due to a rumor Evangel was closing. He ran the race as president all the way to the very end just as any respectable leader would do. Dr. J. Robert Ashcroft was born on December 18, 1911, and passed away on January 5, 1995.

Dr. Robert H. Spence Presidency (1974 – 2014)

Soon after Dr. Ashcroft submitted his resignation, the search began for the next president of Evangel. The board invited many different constituencies to contribute to the type of individual who should be considered. The faculty contributed seven points of guidelines for the board to consider for the new president. Among them were the ability to communicate with various publics, and that the president would ideally hold an earned doctorate ([Faculty Meeting Minutes], 1974). Regardless, the faculty expressed that they would support the final decision of the board of directors and were grateful for the opportunity to contribute to the guidelines. While 21 nominees were considered for the position, the board of directors would ultimately select one of their own.

On March 1, 1974, the official press release announcing Robert H. Spence as the third president of Evangel College after being unanimously elected by the board of directors. His first five-year term was set to begin on May 1, 1974. He was meant to intentionally overlap with outgoing President Ashcroft to facilitate a smooth transition. The bio from his inauguration program was listed as follows:

Robert H. Spence was born in McComb, Mississippi, the son of the Rev. and Mrs. T. H. Spence. Growing up in Montgomery, Ala., Robert Spence enrolled at the University of Alabama. He received his B.A. degree in history and was married to Margaret Anne Tindol in the same year, 1956. They now have three children, Jonathan, age ten; David, age five; and Stephen, age two.

Ordained by the Alabama District Council of the Assemblies of God in 1958, the Rev. Mr. Robert H. Spence has held pastorates in Marion, Ala.; Tuscaloosa, Ala.; and Mobile, Ala. He continued his education, receiving an M.A. degree in school administration in 1959. He has taught in the public schools of Tuscaloosa, Ala., including three years' service as the principal of a junior high school.

In his most recent pastorate, that of the Crichton Assembly of God, Mobile, Ala, the Rev. Mr. Spence developed a Christian day school with grades from kindergarten through twelfth grade. In addition, the Rev. Mr. Spence served the Alabama District as a district presbyter for seven years. He was also campus director of the Mobile extension of South-Eastern Bible College.

The Rev. Mr. Spence was appointed a member of the Evangel College Board of Directors in 1968. He was asked to accept the presidency of the college early in 1974 and assumed office on May 1. His appointment to the office was made by the College Board of Directors and ratified by the Executive Presbytery of the Assemblies of God ([Inauguration Program], 1974, p. 3).

Inauguration

President Spence's inauguration did not occur until the conclusion of his first full semester as president. On December 11, 1974, President Spence was inaugurated as the third president of Evangel. In his inaugural address, he recounted the historical significance of what occurred 20 years prior almost to the day. On December 13, 1954, the land where Evangel sits was officially granted to the Assemblies of God for the development of the university. He also shared of the many developments that had occurred in 20 short years: the first graduating class, accreditation, a library, an activities center, and several residence halls. He said, "Developing in an atmosphere of miracles, the miraculous became a way of life for the college" ([Inauguration Address], 1974, p. 3).

Spence went on to explain his understanding that "... education without a spiritual perspective is minus its most essential element" ([Inauguration Address], 1974, p. 4). To him, Evangel's finest hour was beginning as he believed there was the opportunity to strive for the highest levels of scholarship with the deepest levels of Christian commitment. Rather than being mutually exclusive, Evangel had the distinct advantage of housing a community of people mutually committed to God and each other within this growing academic enterprise ([Inauguration Address], 1974). Spence concluded his inaugural address with an acceptance of the charge laid before him. He said, "And so to the Board of Directors, the faculty, and staff, and the students, I dedicate myself as a servant, accepting the responsibility as president of Evangel College, and shall strive to fulfill it to the best of my ability and to the glory of God" ([Inauguration Address], 1974, p. 7). History would show that he would carry on that dedication for the next 40 years.

Operations of the College

Months before his official inauguration, and even weeks before he officially took office, President Spence was already beginning his work. His first official meeting with the faculty in the capacity of president took place on April 10, 1974. He shared a brief introduction that was followed by a question and answer session with the 62 faculty who were present. He would also almost immediately begin collaborating with Dr. Ashcroft on a spring fundraising campaign to assist in making up for a shortcoming in meeting projected fundraising revenues. President Spence's self-sacrificial leadership began long before his tenure as president did.

It was again exhibited in an anecdotal story about a controversy involving personal investments he made in a local banking institution for which he served on the board. In a meeting with faculty, and with follow up correspondence, he indicates that, due to negative media attention from investments he had made in good faith, he would be divesting himself from his investments and stepping down from his position on the board of the bank. "I am confident that this decision to remove myself entirely from any connection with the bank is in the best interest of the church, the college, and the bank" (Spence, 1977, p. 1). Divesting oneself from totally legitimate investments for the benefit of the institution that is served is an extraordinary display of self-sacrificial leadership.

The relationship and collaboration between Dr. Ashcroft and President Spence actually began years before the presidential transition when Spence was the president of Chi Alpha at the University of Alabama. In 1957, Spence invited Ashcroft to be the Chi Alpha representative and stayed with the Spences for one week while ministering to college students (Spence, 2005). In June of 1963, then Rev. Spence would inquire of Dr.

Ashcroft for career advice on a best course of action related to a graduate degree. Spence was being encouraged by a former professor to pursue a Ph.D., and he sought Ashcroft's advice by asking, "In light of your experience and the present trend in our fellowship, do you think this would be a wise course of action?" (Spence, 1963, p. 1). In Dr. Ashcroft's response, he encourages him to consider a Ph.D. in a specific field other than education "…were you to think of serving Evangel College" (Ashcroft, 1963, p. 1). At the time, Evangel was drawing near to accreditation and greatly in need of professors with Ph.D. degrees in specialized fields. Just a few years later, Spence would join the board and begin working with Ashcroft even more closely in that capacity.

In the spring of 1974 during the transition in presidential leadership, Ashcroft was working to leave a firm foundation from which Spence could launch his presidency. Ashcroft had many different courses he could have taken to finish his final academic year. He chose to ensure a smooth transition, and he made Spence aware of a change in the fiscal affairs of the institution due to the rumors that had been previously mentioned. In a memo on April 3, 1974, he clearly indicates the factors he believes were involved and the actions he plans to take. He ends his note to Spence and General Council leadership, with positivity by stating one of the bright spots was to have a new president "with youth and leadership to stimulate new sources of additional major gifts and support" (Ashcroft, 1974, April 3, p. 1).

Later in the summer of 1974, one of the first pieces of correspondence President Spence sends after the close of the fiscal year is a thank you note with an update to Dr. Ashcroft. In it he shares that the operations of the 73-74 fiscal year ended in the black. This is quite miraculous considering this was a year of presidential transition, the shortage that was projected for the fiscal year, and the drastic drop in donations the administration was seeing in the spring due to the transition (Spence, 1974). The surplus of $13,624 was absorbed by the beginning deficit of the year, but Spence still makes a point to celebrate and express gratitude for Ashcroft's work and leadership. He says:

> After carrying this burden for so many years and especially during these past months, I know that this is an answer to your prayers. I just wanted to extend this note of appreciation for your work and concern that made this victory possible. (Spence, 1974, p. 1).

A day before his note to Dr. Ashcroft, President Spence again expressed gratitude and gave credit to Dr. Ashcroft in his report to the General Presbytery. In this first report to the General Presbytery as president, Spence shared his concept of Evangel to be "that of a school owned and operated by the Assemblies of God, staffed with the most proficient and well-prepared faculty, housed in the most adequate facilities, and enjoying total compatibility with our fellowship" ([General Presbytery Report], 1974, p. 2) After softly mentioning the continued need for facility development, Spence would request two areas of support from the General Presbytery in his first report. He requested assistance in communicating with the denominational churches the importance of making Evangel a part of their monthly missionary support. He saw Evangel as an arm of the AG serving a missional role, and thus missional support from the churches should be encouraged.

He also requested a review of the proclamation from a year before when this same body took the position that no capital expense would be approved until the accounts were brought back into balance. He agreed with the position, but he also asked for quarterly consideration with the focus of reactivating the chapel building fund that had begun several years prior. His main capital focus was on the development of the chapel building. Several other buildings would also come into development as the deficit was relieved. This was in large part thanks to the addition of football to the athletic offerings of the school. As a graduate of the University of Alabama, President Spence certainly saw firsthand how a thriving football program could benefit a college.

Dr. David Stair, longtime Athletic Director at Evangel, first joined as a faculty member for the Physical Education department in 1976. At his retirement in 2014, he compiled a history of athletics and physical education at Evangel. In it, he recounts the success of several athletic teams during the 60s and 70s, and he provides a brief review of the founding of football at Evangel.

In November of 1974, the first year of the Spence presidency, students from Evangel and Central Bible College played the first annual CBC vs. Evangel football classic (Stair, 2014). Evangel won the game 12-0. That same academic year in April of 1975, Evangel played Baptist Bible College in a full-pad football scrimmage with Evangel winning that contest 12-6 (Stair, 2014).

In the fall of 1976, President Spence announced that Evangel would begin its inaugural football season the following year. He also announced that former football star and well-known evangelist Denny Duron would take the helm as the very first head coach. Duron had spoken at Evangel during a spiritual emphasis week, and President Spence asked him to pray about becoming the first head coach. Duron agreed and brought a perspective of using football as a ministry. With the addition of football, the study body enrollment saw a significant spike and the university had to make unique housing plans as the decade turned to accommodate the growth.

In the early years, the football program was housed in the Public Relations department under the direction of Neil Eskelin, Director of Development at the time (Stair, 2014). The team was not affiliated with a conference so they would agree to play anyone willing to add them to their schedule. The team would play on Saturday, and the PR department would help them identify a church for ministry in the locale of the game the following Sunday. Members of the team formed a choir, players would share testimonies, and Coach Duron would speak (Stair, 2014). With Eskelin's expertise and Duron's charismatic personality, there came the production of a syndicated weekly hour-long highlight TV Show produced by local NBC affiliate in Springfield, KY3 (Stair, 2014). The hope was for Evangel to become the Notre Dame of the AG and Pentecostals at large.

The players who were part of the team during Coach Duron's tenure as coach, from 1977 to 1982, have been named the "Originals." A significant event, often discussed and referred to by many of the Originals, was the game against the large local public state institution in Springfield, Southwest Missouri State (SMS, now Missouri State University). In the second season of existence, fall of 1978, the Evangel football team defeated SMS 33 – 21.

While the founding of the football program was the first major initiative completed by President Spence, several successful building programs followed as enrollment and fundraising began to increase.

1978 – BURGESS HALL: This four-story residence hall is named for Doyle E. Burgess, a former member of the Board of Directors and a president of the Council. Burgess Hall can house 288 students.

1980 – LEWIS HALL: The largest of the residence halls, this four-story facility can house 352 students. It was named for Gayle F. Lewis, former general superintendent of the Assemblies of God.

1981 – THE ROBERT H. SPENCE CHAPEL: The 2,170-seat chapel is the central the spiritual life of our campus. In 1994, the Evangel College Board of Directors named the chapel for then-President Robert H. Spence, but at his request, his name was not placed on the building until his retirement in 2014. The stained-glass windows were donated by Mr. Earl Fester in memory of his wife, Mary Elizabeth. (Note: Opened for fall 1981, dedicated April 2, 1982). (Logsdon, 2018, pp. 2-3).

It should be noted that the building of the chapel was included despite being completed after the first 25 years because of how long that project had been in process. However, there were significant funding challenges related to the building of Lewis Hall and the Chapel. These should be included in a follow up research on the next 25 years of the institution's existence so an analysis of the impact on the school can be examined.

Enrollment trends, tuition charges, fundraising success, and total income are all important data points for any president.

Pioneering Spirit

Figure 7

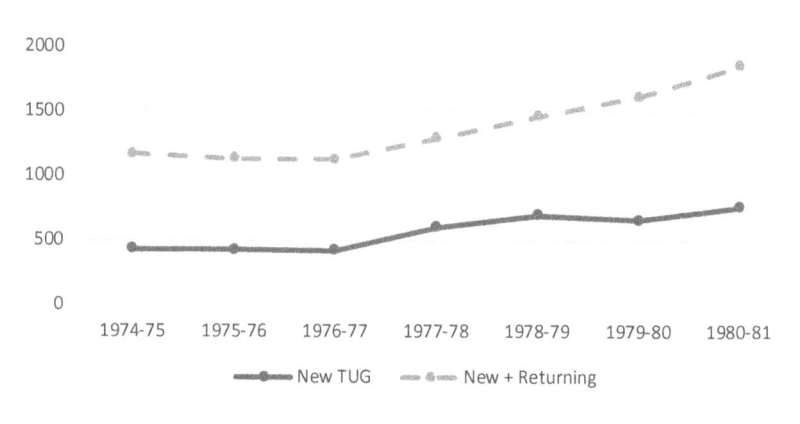

Spence Presidency Enrollment Trend

While President Spence completed a 40-year term as president, only his first seven years are included here to stay within the timeframe being studied. Enrollment trended upward for the beginning of his tenure. His first major initiative was to start the football program in 1977. We do see an increase in enrollment for that year.

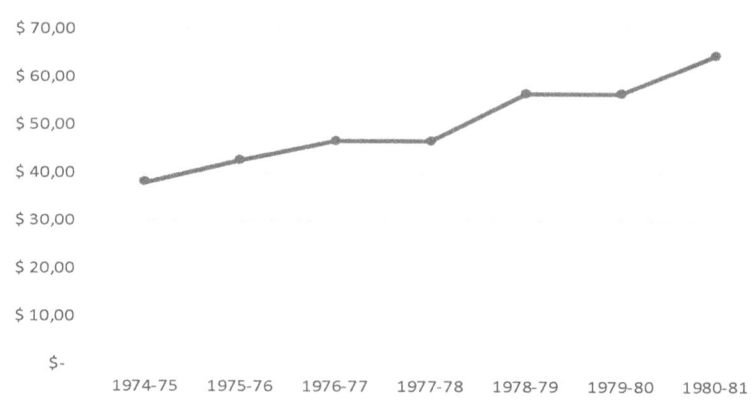

Figure 8

Spence Presidency - Tuition Per Hour Cost Trend

Contributions, tuition income, and total income are important pieces of data of the first few years of Spence's presidency.

Figure 9

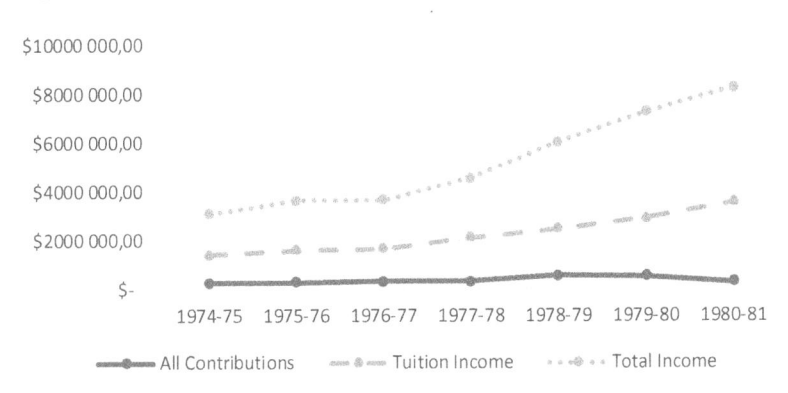

Spence Presidency - Contributions, Enrollment Income, Total Income

Dr. Spence was born on September 13, 1935, and passed away on February 19, 2020.

Summary

To this point, key data points for each individual president have been shared, and it would be appropriate to consider the comprehensive data points for the first quarter century of the institution's existence. Enrollment generally trended upward during this timeframe as seen in Figure 10.

Figure 10

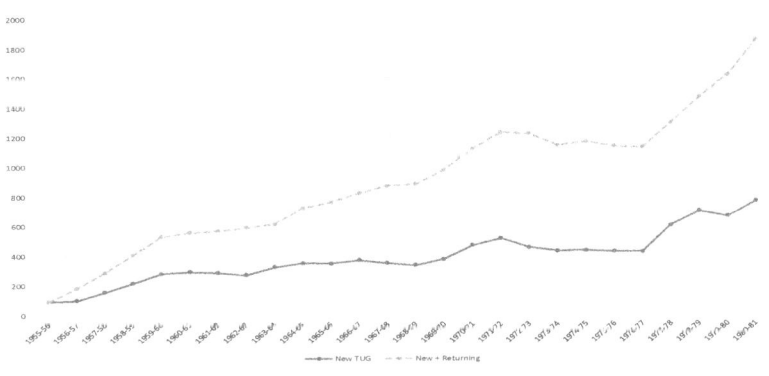

First 25 Years Enrollment Trend - 1955-1980

Pioneering Spirit

Figure 11 shows the cost trend of tuition during the first 25 years.

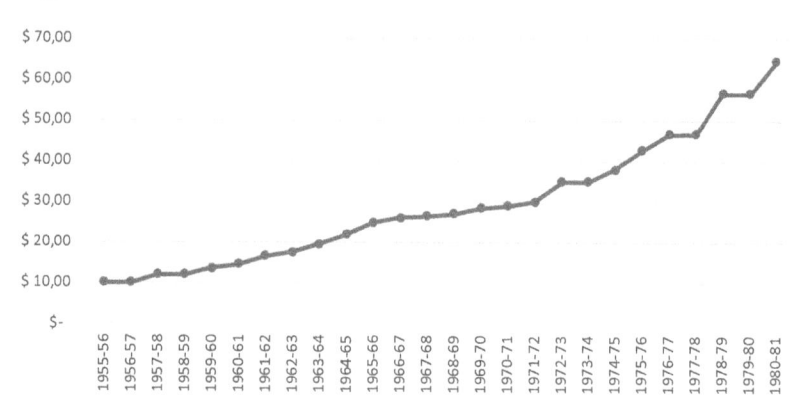

Figure 11

First 25 Years - Tuition Per Hour Cost

Putting all the contributions, tuition income, and total income together over the first 25 years shows, in Figure 12, how significant the growth in total income was correlating with the beginning of the football program. Interestingly, contributions did not rise significantly and decreased at the end.

Figure 12

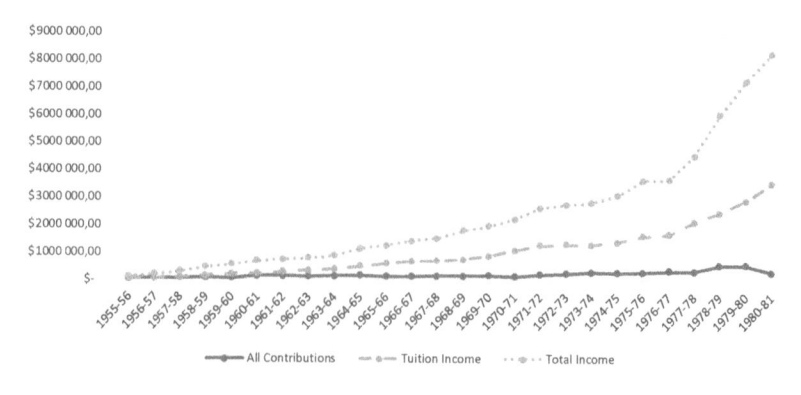

First 25 Years - Contributions, Enrollment Income, Total Income

The first 25 years of the institution saw an incredible amount of transition. This chapter intends to serve as a broad review of those years focused on the presidents who lead during that time and the characteristics they exhibited. The intent is for this chapter to serve as a compilation of the key parts of the history that will inspire future researchers to add depth to different components of the institution's history. While serving as a review, there are also several important themes that emerged from the research.

From before the institution began, there was a persistence from Ralph Riggs that helped establish an important part of the ethos of the institution. In competitive terms, he showed a willingness to do whatever it took to "win." In his mind, winning was establishing the first Pentecostal liberal arts institution in the country. He won, even at the detriment to his own career. This, too, became a part of the early years of the institution. It is defined here as self-sacrificial leadership, a willingness to sacrifice one's own ambitions or desires for the benefit of those being served.

Riggs sacrificed his career to establish Evangel. Kendrick sacrificed his presidency to assist in implementing the first consolidation of Evangel and CBI which he felt would improve the financial condition of the institution. Ashcroft sacrificed his presidency for what he felt was best for the future of Evangel, and he sacrificed his own ego to establish a smooth transition and strong beginning for the next president. Spence sacrificed his own personal investments to avoid bringing negative attention to the institution.

Faculty and staff followed the lead of each president in making sacrifices in their own ways. Many sacrificed career advancement and financial development to follow each president in executing the mission of the university. Many faculty sacrificed opportunities to write and research to spend more time investing directly in the lives of the students they taught. Some sacrificed their health, like Dr. Williams and his asthma, to meet the challenge of their specific time and purpose.

Finally, the students were impacted by this type of leadership as all of them made a sacrifice in the first ten years by attending an unaccredited institution whose future was largely unknown. The Pioneers, those who attended in the first ten years of the school's existence, established this idea of self-sacrifice amongst the students. This was evident for so many who sacrificed comfortable living arrangements other institutions might have offered to stay in worn down army barracks.

The barracks provided close contact and intimate quarters for residents and faculty alike. Rooms were small, offices were small, and the hallways, that ran from one end of the campus to the other in a grid-like fashion as indicated in Figure 13, were narrow and small.

Figure 13

Aerial Shot of Evangel College Campus, circa 1955

The hallways used to navigate the institution during the first 25 years were narrow and forced community through proximity.

Figure 14

Interior of Barracks Hallway

Even while permanent buildings were being erected, the barracks remained an integral part of the infrastructure of the campus during the first 25 years and beyond.

Figure 15

Aerial Shot of Evangel College Campus, circa 1980

When discussing spiritual development, understanding of calling, or integration of faith and learning, the students at the time would have to engage intentionally and proactively to receive those experiences. If they did not desire development in their faith or calling, then they would not have received the shared experience that many others did. However, the students had no choice when it came to the barracks. That was a shared experience that was forced upon every student who lived and learned at Evangel, and in the early years, many faculty who lived in the barracks as well. The barracks as a shared experience transcended time, age, major, background, spiritual growth, and any other differentiating characteristic. The barracks created the space for the deep, meaningful relationships so prevalent in the responses in interviews and surveys and created a continuity of experience that has bonded students and alumni who share it. The barracks, as austere as they were, had a way of removing the distractions that could have existed in more comfortable or lavish circumstances.

Figure 16

Campus Shot of Barracks

These sacrifices speak highly of the type of atmosphere and total learning environment that was experienced by those who attended, matriculated, and eventually graduated. The distinctive element of Evangel outweighed the physical and facility limitations that were so evident. So many alumni have indicated that their experience did not feel like a sacrifice in the least when they considered the impact the professors of the institution made on their lives, the development of their faith that occurred, the preparation for careers they experienced, and the relationships they gained which have spanned the decades since they were on campus. The impact of self-sacrificial leadership on subordinates is further explored and discussed in Chapter 6.

The political frame of organizations developed by Bolman and Deal (2013) proposes that "...interdependence, divergent interests, scarcity, and power relations inevitably spawn political activity" (p. 188). This frame utilized five assumptions to summarize the perspective:

- Organizations are coalitions of different individuals and interest groups.
- Coalition members have enduring differences in values, beliefs, information, interests, and perceptions of reality.
- Most important decisions involve allocating scarce resources.
- Scarce resources and enduring differences put conflict at the center of day-to-day dynamics and make power the most important asset.
- Goals and decisions emerge from bargaining and negotiation among competing stakeholders jockeying for their own interests. (Bolman and Deal, 2013, pp. 188-189)

Colleges and universities are arenas that are often cited as being political ecosystems where resolving conflict, utilizing power, and building coalitions are dynamic and complex. When discussing higher education institutions, it is said they have "... lived through alternating eras of feast and famine related to peaks and valleys of economic and demographic trends" (Bolman and Deal, 2013, p.190). A hallmark of successful navigation through the political environment of any organizations has everything to do with developing effective and strategic relationships. The role of power is an important factor leaders must consider when working to move an organization forward. Whether power is positional, coercive, informational, expertise, reputational, or referent, a good leader will understand the ebb and flow of power, its effect on important relationships, and how it can be utilized to benefit the organization. "Managers often fail to get things done because they rely too much on reason and too little on relationships" (Bolman and Deal, 2013, p. 212).

In addition to the politics that impacted Evangel in its early years, state and federal politics also played an important role in its development. Since before its founding, Evangel and denominational leaders have developed strong relationships with local, state, and federal representatives that have been largely beneficial to the institution. From assisting with getting the land needed for a campus to helping achieve regional accreditation politics of all kinds have played a crucial role in the institution's success.

The subsequent 25 years would see its own laundry list of challenges and opportunities that included significant enrollment uncertainty, unprecedented athletic success, the advent of the internet, a major campus facility transformation, and the explosion of the technological age.

Chapter 5 will reveal the presentation of findings and the process and methodology that was utilized to garner widespread feedback from alumni who lived the history shared in this chapter. Their feedback and experiences provide individual historical accounts and aggregated historical data that complements this historical narrative.

CHAPTER FIVE
PRESENTATION OF FINDINGS

Introduction

Leadership in the first years of any organization is pivotal to its success. The purpose of this study is to explore by synthesizing common themes derived from firsthand accounts of Evangel alumni, former professors, and administrators who lived the history during the period being studied into a historical narrative. The work builds on Corey's (1993) dissertation and Corey's (2005) historical narrative detailing the founding of the institution. An additional purpose of the collective narrative is to identify events, experiences, and strategies that contributed to the institutional persistence, academic preparation, and flourishing faith integration that characterized the Evangel University experience since its founding in 1955.

Data collection began by interviewing alumni, former school leaders, and former faculty to gather perceptions of their experiences at Evangel. Interview data were collected and compiled to assist in identifying the emerging themes from the lived experiences of alumni, former leaders, and former faculty. These interviews contributed to the creation of a survey that was used to collect feedback from a broad cross-section of alumni who attended the institution during the first 25 years. Additionally, archival data were reviewed to identify common themes regarding the tenure of three different presidents who served Evangel during the first 25 years. The archival data collection included the investigation of the following documents:

- Transcripts of previously recorded oral histories
- Data compiled and utilized for prior research
- Presidential speech transcripts
- Presidential articles
- Faculty and staff meeting minutes and notes
- Correspondence between leaders
- Other archival material.

Both the archival material review and the alumni interviews and subsequent surveys were done to address the central question of the research. The central question is:

> What practices from the first 25 years of Evangel University can be applied to positive, successful mission fulfillment in the future?

These practices can be identified through careful analysis of the alumni survey and interview responses as well as archival data research. To effectively move forward, any organization must have an accurate understanding of its history and how that history has contributed to its current context.

The additional research questions that were addressed through the research were as follows:

Presentation of Findings

1. How do alumni perceive the spiritual development they experienced while at Evangel University impacted their personal and professional lives?
2. What experiences do alumni, faculty, and staff from the first 25 years share from their time at Evangel?
3. From the perspective of faculty, staff, and alumni, what historical events during the first 25 years of Evangel University's existence shaped the foundational ethos of the institution?
4. Which themes emerge when alumni reflect upon their respective careers and contexts?

Data Collection

Three main sources of data were collected and analyzed for this study. First, more than 40 one-to-one personal interviews were conducted. These interviews provided subjective and anecdotal evidence of experiences and perceptions related to the research questions being addressed. Second, a survey based on the examination of the interview responses was created to collect additional information from a broader cross-section of alumni. Third, historical documents were reviewed to address research questions including board meeting minutes, press releases, oral histories, and archival documents. These documents were accessed in the university archives with the assistance of the volunteer archivist for the university. Much of the data was collected as part of the researcher's professional responsibilities at the university. A review of the protocols for collecting, analysis of the data, and interpretation of the findings will explore results from the survey first to show the breadth of data revealing the experience of alumni. Second, the personal interviews will show the depth of the experience through personal and anecdotal evidence. Third, the historical documents will provide the historical context and support for the experiences of participants in the study.

Identification of Participants

Because of the historical nature of this research, the participants for this study were former administrators, faculty, staff, and alumni from 1955 to 1980. Alumni who were involved in the research, whether through emails or surveys, covered each year of existence in the first 25 years of the university. Some individuals participated in the personal interview stage, some participated in the survey stage, and some participated in both.

Participant Survey Protocol

The survey was sent to all alumni, for whom a valid email address was accessible, across the 25-year period being researched along with multiple reminders. Email addresses of alumni who fit this demographic were identified through the alumni database in the Evangel University Advancement office. An initial email invitation to participate in the survey was sent with two follow-up reminder emails across a four-week period. Three emails were sent to invite completion of the survey. The first email was sent to 1,652 recipients and had a 51.2% open rate. The second email was sent to 1,641 recipients and had a 46.4% open rate. The third email was sent to 1,643 recipients and had a 45.1% open rate. The survey received 387 responses resulting in an approximate response rate of 24%. This was calculated by dividing the number of responses by the average number of recipients across the three emails. Copies of the invitation emails can be found in Appendix E.

Presentation of Findings

One-to-One Interview Protocol

Interviewees were purposefully selected based on recommendations from individuals with strong historical knowledge of the institution and the researcher's experience with participants. Additionally, pre-recorded interviews and oral histories already available in the archives of the university were examined for this study. Participants were invited for interviews via email or phone call. Some of the interviews were conducted in person and recorded using a handheld recording device. In some cases, a video conferencing tool was used to record the discussion. In other instances, the interviews were conducted via phone call, and the handheld recording device was used while the phone call was on the speaker phone setting. Interviewees selected the setting for the interviews and were informed that the interviews would be recorded.

Historical Document Data Collection Protocol

To begin this historical analysis of the institution, a review of relevant documents from the first 25 years was conducted. A search was conducted through all available documentation in the university archives from 1955 to 1980. These documents included charter documents, board minutes, academic program files, other historical narratives, research collected and conducted by Corey (1993), and oral histories from key personnel in leadership. In addition, documents located in the Flower Pentecostal Heritage Center at the Assemblies of God National Office were reviewed. Some of those documents were available on-site and some were only available in the organization's online collection.

Pioneering Spirit

Data Analysis

Data analysis began with a review of the recorded interviews. Additionally, survey responses were charted and categorically analyzed. Interview and survey data were compared, and emergent themes were triangulated with data collected from historical documents. The following sections provide a detailed description of the procedures used to conduct the survey, interview, and document data analysis.

Participant Survey Data Analysis

Survey data analysis was done to reveal trends in the experiences and perceptions of the respondents. The information compiled was utilized to assist in answering the appropriate research questions of the study. As responses to interviews and surveys were collected, these subjective experiences were compared to objective data like enrollment, campus development projects, budget issues, and other key events that may have been connected to the experiences of the participants.

Figure 17 reveals that, of the 387 responses received through the survey, 53.76% were female and 46.24% were male.

Figure 17

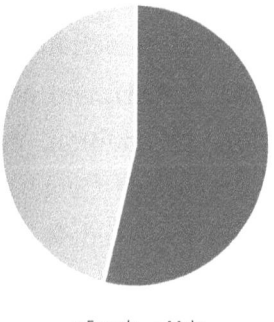

Survey Participant Gender

Presentation of Findings

In his research, Strahan (1955) estimated the populations of the towns from which Evangel students would come to be between 5,000 and 50,000. Data collected in this study supported the accuracy of Strahan's prediction. Figure 18 illustrates that the majority of survey respondents (58.3%) reported the population size of their hometowns to be between 1 and 50,000 people.

Figure 18

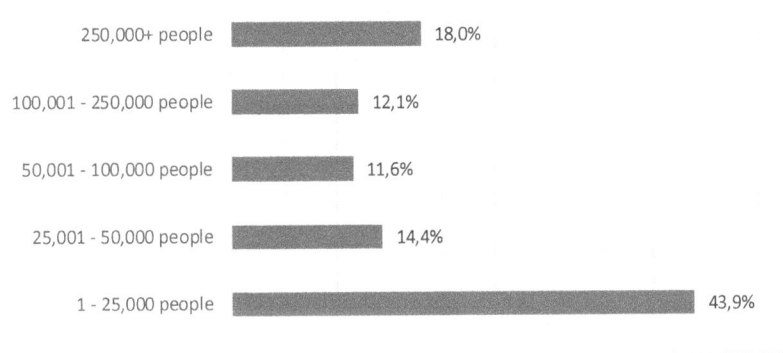

Home Town Size	Percentage
250,000+ people	18.0%
100,001 - 250,000 people	12.1%
50,001 - 100,000 people	11.6%
25,001 - 50,000 people	14.4%
1 - 25,000 people	43.9%

Home Town Size

Another important component to review from the participants is what variables were most impactful on their decision to attend Evangel. Figure 19 reveals the average scores and rankings delivered on a variety of variables. Survey participants were asked to rank factors from 1 (not important) to 10 (most important). The affiliation with the AG ranked the highest in importance with an average score of 8.02. The academic major averaged 7.36 and ranked second in importance with accreditation ranking third with an average of 6.87. Interestingly, the president's identity was ranked second from the bottom at 3.99. Considering how highly presidents were admired according to interview and open-ended survey responses, this

Pioneering Spirit

is a surprising finding. The finding indicates that the president may not have had a strong influence on recruiting students to the institution but played a strong role in retention and student satisfaction once the students arrived on campus.

Figure 19

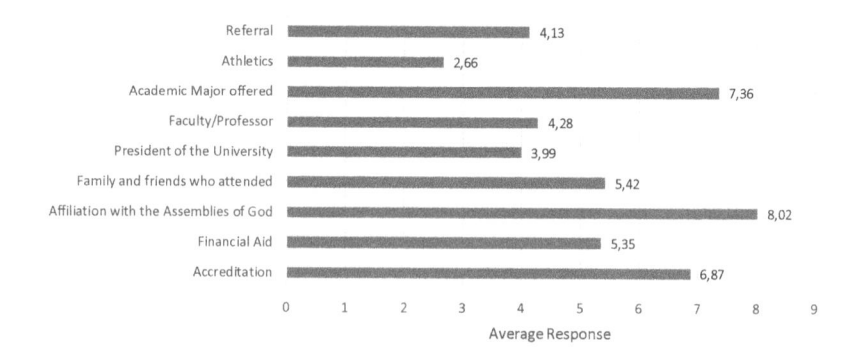

Category	Average Response
Referral	4,13
Athletics	2,66
Academic Major offered	7,36
Faculty/Professor	4,28
President of the University	3,99
Family and friends who attended	5,42
Affiliation with the Assemblies of God	8,02
Financial Aid	5,35
Accreditation	6,87

Impact on Decision to Attend Evangel
(1=not important; 10=extremely important)

From the beginning, part of the mission of Evangel was to perpetuate the Pentecostal tradition of the AG. According to Figure 20, 83.5% of respondents strongly agreed or somewhat agreed that Evangel was successful in this part of the mission.

Figure 20

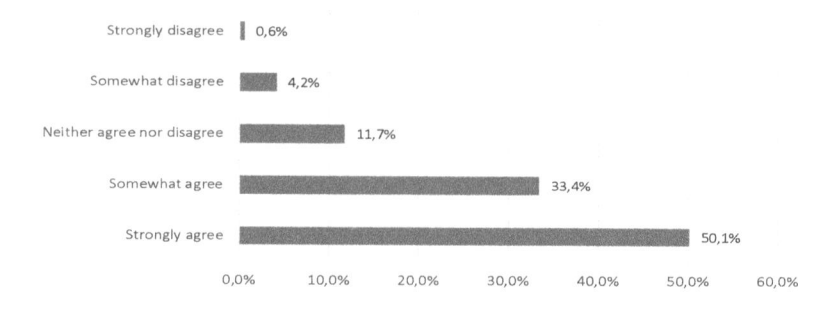

Response	Percentage
Strongly disagree	0,6%
Somewhat disagree	4,2%
Neither agree nor disagree	11,7%
Somewhat agree	33,4%
Strongly agree	50,1%

Evangel has been successful in perpetuating
the Pentecostal tradition of the AG.

In addition to perpetuating the Pentecostal traditions of the AG, Evangel also provided an integral higher education experience for students interested in vocations outside of full-time vocational ministry. Figure 21 shows that 98% of respondents strongly agreed or somewhat agreed that Evangel successfully fulfilled that part of the mission.

Figure 21

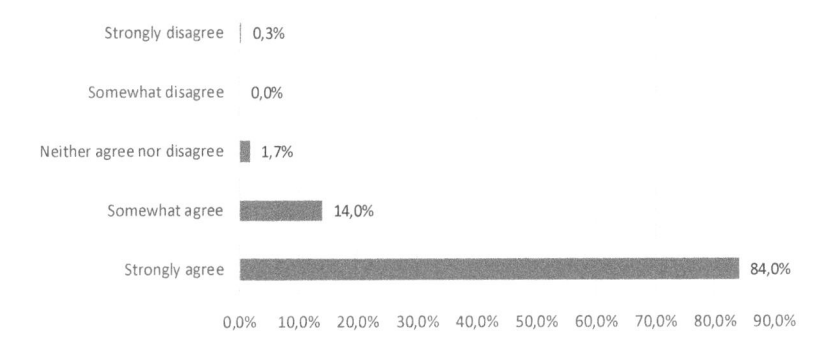

Response	Percentage
Strongly disagree	0,3%
Somewhat disagree	0,0%
Neither agree nor disagree	1,7%
Somewhat agree	14,0%
Strongly agree	84,0%

Evangel has provided higher education for students who were called in areas outside of vocational church ministry.

Figure 22 shows 76% of respondents strongly agreed or somewhat agreed that perpetuating the AG as a denomination should be a part of the mission of the institution. More will be discussed when evaluating the percentage of respondents who still consider themselves adherents to the AG tradition later in the analysis of the data collected.

Figure 22

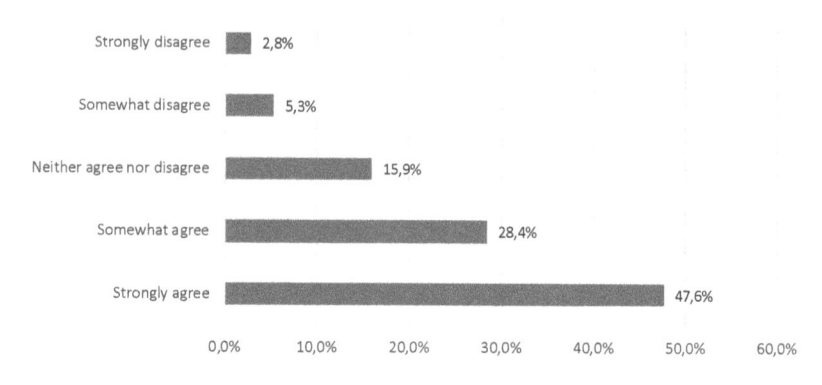

Strongly disagree	2,8%
Somewhat disagree	5,3%
Neither agree nor disagree	15,9%
Somewhat agree	28,4%
Strongly agree	47,6%

The university mission should include perpetuating the AG as a fellowship.

One-to-One Interview Data Analysis

Recorded personal interviews were reviewed to analyze responses in relation to the research questions. Many of the recorded interviews were transcribed to carefully review responses and identify themes through common word searches in the transcriptions. Interviews were coded based on the interviewee's role at the institution during the time period being studied. Some interviewees were students, faculty, and administrators during that timeframe. Care was taken to focus on the role that was most relevant for the individual during the first 25 years of Evangel's existence.

Those who were students during that time were coded as S (for student) and then given a number based on the order in which the interviews were conducted (i.e., S1, S2, S3, etc.). Those who were faculty or administrators during that time were coded as L (for leader) and assigned a number based on the order in which the interviews were conducted (i.e., L1, L2, L3, etc.). Some interview participants were students, then later became leaders. In those instances, participants were asked to consider their responses from their student perspectives. In some cases, multiple individuals were involved in the same interview. This occurred when married couples or siblings were interviewed at the same time. In those instances, an added element to coding included a decimal point and a number to represent which of the interviewees was speaking (i.e., SI.1, SI.2, etc.). Repeated words and phrases were noted to identify patterns in the data. As patterns were identified, survey questions were designed to collect similar objective data from a larger sample of the target population.

Historical Document Data Analysis

From the analysis of historical documents, a focus was placed on key events between 1955 and 1980. These included gaining accreditation, presidential transitions, and the construction of permanent buildings. The focus of the historical data analysis was to discover the leadership traits and qualities of the presidents from the first 25 years of the university. Data collected from the documents were then compared to the interview and survey responses to identify how key events may have contributed to the growth of the university and the execution of its mission during its founding years.

Research Questions

After establishing the central question that guided the study, there were four sub-questions that helped clarify the purpose of the study. For each sub-question, an analysis of the survey response data, interview response data, and historical document data will follow.

Research Sub-Question 1

How do alumni perceive the spiritual development they

experienced while at Evangel University impacted their personal and professional lives? The first research sub-question was addressed by survey, interview, and historical document data.

Major Influences on Spiritual Development

Questions regarding spiritual development were taken from an annual survey utilized most recently to quantify the spiritual development that occurs in students' spiritual lives while enrolled at Evangel. To provide comparable data to the experience of alumni from the first 25 years the same or similar questions were used for this survey. Figure 23 shows how respondents answered the survey item regarding who provided the biggest influence on their spiritual growth while they were a student at Evangel. The top five responses reported to have the biggest influence on the spiritual growth of the respondent were friends (24.8%), professors (18.3%), yourself (14.3%), campus pastor (13%), and parents (9.3%).

Figure 23

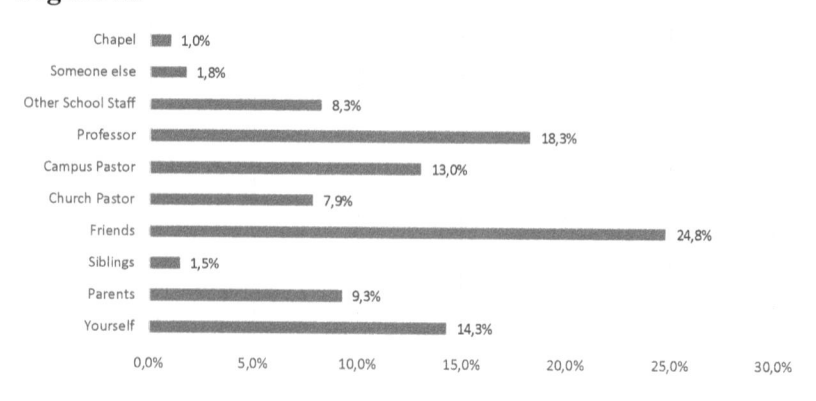

Category	Percentage
Chapel	1.0%
Someone else	1.8%
Other School Staff	8.3%
Professor	18.3%
Campus Pastor	13.0%
Church Pastor	7.9%
Friends	24.8%
Siblings	1.5%
Parents	9.3%
Yourself	14.3%

Biggest Influence on Spiritual Growth

Impact of Faculty Role Models

Faculty members serving as role models is certainly a common theme mentioned in the survey responses. According to survey results, professors provided the second biggest influence on the respondents' spiritual growth after their friends. One respondent summarized:

> It would be hard to separate out one or two [faculty members]. The faculty and staff were so few, and we all interacted closely. But I would say Bernard Bresson, Richard Strahan, and Klaude Kendrick [stand out] in terms of spurring academic interest and generally modeling the idea that one could be a Christian and still be academically curious.

While it was mentioned by participants that faculty quality varied, the majority of faculty exhibited substantial self-sacrificial leadership simply by agreeing to teach at Evangel. Salary data from the early years is an indication of the sacrifice faculty members made to be part of the Evangel community as early teachers were paid $3,000 to $4,000 per year. Comparatively, a survey of practices of AG colleges from 1968 revealed that the average salary for a full professor was between $7,661 and $9,605 ([Survey of Practices], 1968). Many survey respondents shared a knowledge and understanding of the self-sacrifice exhibited by faculty and staff just to be at Evangel serving the students and carrying out the mission.

A special evening faculty meeting held on April 1, 1958, revealed poignantly how important the spiritual development of the student body was of utmost importance for the faculty and administration from the very beginning. Nearly 80% of the faculty at the time were involved in the meeting that was focused on how to address a spiritual apathy that was being seen in the students at the time. Genuine concern was expressed, and remarks by the faculty revealed how deeply they cared for the souls of their students.

Results of Evangel Impact

When asked to rate each statement that began with the phrase, "My Evangel experience...", the highest rated of the list of average responses was that Evangel "provided meaningful relationships which impacted my life" (8.94). One survey respondent supported the importance of relationships formed during this time by stating, "A president who inspired me and always knew my name [was] J. Robert Ashcroft." The second highest response was that Evangel "revealed teachers/faculty who modeled and reinforced how to grow spiritually" (8.2). The experience that Evangel provided adequate academic preparation in the classroom was also highly ranked (8.17). Interestingly, one of the lowest scores of 7.87 was given for the statement, "Evangel contributed to my spiritual formation and development." One survey responder added succinctly, "Evangel was where I began to understand with my head what I felt in my heart and became a defender of my faith." Figure 24 represents participants' responses to this survey item.

Figure 24

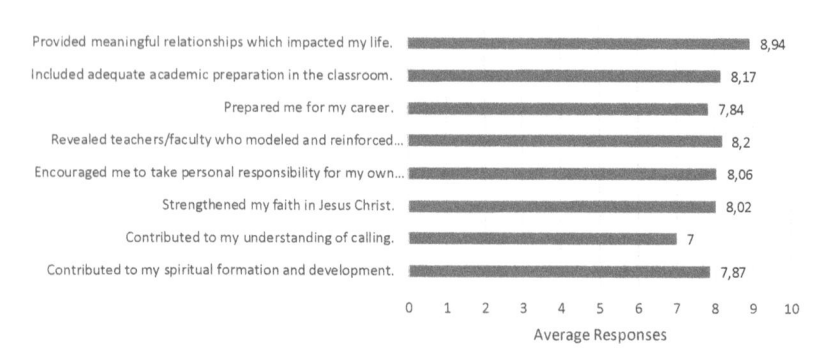

Statement	Average
Provided meaningful relationships which impacted my life.	8,94
Included adequate academic preparation in the classroom.	8,17
Prepared me for my career.	7,84
Revealed teachers/faculty who modeled and reinforced...	8,2
Encouraged me to take personal responsibility for my own...	8,06
Strengthened my faith in Jesus Christ.	8,02
Contributed to my understanding of calling.	7
Contributed to my spiritual formation and development.	7,87

Average Responses

My Evangel experience...
(statements rated 1 = minimum - 10 = maximum)

Sense of Unity

A review of the personal interviews with alumni and leaders revealed a depth of experience that supports the findings of the broader survey. "It definitely was faith-based, [with students] all moving in the same direction, but I never ever felt alone" (SI1). This experience was common for students across the quarter-century time span. There was an obvious faith component that was experienced, and students felt a sense of being "in this together." At the very least they characterized the experience with others around them as "moving in the same direction." While it is understood that these statements were generalities and it is recognized that not all students were affected by or interested in the faith culture on campus, data indicates the majority were. For example, SI2.1 noted,

> It definitely was a oneness. You are not just a part of a few, you are part of everybody, and everybody was so open. You talked to somebody and they already shared your same ideas and already shared the same way of looking at things and it brought you into close unity with everybody there, and I don't know how you would have that if you were in an unbelieving group. So being a born-again Christian made a huge difference because you know one another because of the Lord, spiritually as well as physically because you are with them.

SI9 agreed, "By attending Evangel, I matured in my walk with Christ, and I believe that was because I was with other young people with the same faith, values and goals in life." SI1 added,

> "I have to tell you that I always felt about Evangel, yes it was faith-based no question, integrated faith and learning, that's all it was then. Wonderful. It is more now. But beyond that additionally, it was a feeling of caring, being mattered."

Pioneering Spirit

Being cared for or seen individually was noted by several participants as a characteristic of the school that helped set the context for the spiritual development that took place.

In response to being cared for and seen on campus, students identified leaders on campus who were caring for them as models to emulate. "They would pray with us when we needed prayer, they were Christian role models for us. We could look up to all of our professors because of the example they led in their own lives," reported SI9. President Robert Spence was often mentioned as an example of a leader to emulate. SI4 expressed:

> I learned at Evangel on multiple occasions how important it was to commit things to prayer, and I had models for that. President Spence probably had more influence on my life than anyone else except for my father. I grew a lot spiritually not only from chapel but just from being around him, so I [hope] that spiritual distinctive is something Evangel never, ever loses.

Another point made by participants was that spiritual development was a naturally occurring aspect of the experience in the classroom. SI1 stated,

> Through Christian eyes, we were learning whatever the class happened to be. That goes back to faith. We touched on everything. Nothing was off limits, but it was through that Christian focus. I will say that there were so many, if not all, of the professor's leadership, I was in the Spence era, and I adored the man.

The context of Evangel helped create the atmosphere for spiritual development to continue to contexts off campus. SI2.3 shared,

> It helped develop my worldview. I was so isolated in that small community that I grew up in; the youth group in our church was 5, four others and myself and it was really sad.

So to get to Evangel and be able to go to those churches that had college groups that were 3 and 4 hundred in one room was amazing and a little overwhelming. It helped me develop a better worldview where a Christian could be and what you could do.

The learning environment described by the participants affected their spiritual development and continues to be cherished by many of them. LI2.2 explained, "To us the knowledge of Christ and committing your life to his service is essential and I hope Evangel will never lose that particular footing."

Historical Document Data

Figure 21 shows the small placard that remained on President Robert Ashcroft's desk throughout his presidency. The placard contained a verse from 2 Chronicles 26:5: "As long as he sought the Lord, God made him to prosper." He was known for using this verse to guide his presidency and began having additional placards made that he could give out to students and faculty and send to others he knew off campus.

Figure 25

Actual Placard from J. Robert Ashcroft's Desk

Research Sub-Question 2

Data from the surveys, interviews, and review of historical documents also addressed the second research question: What experiences do alumni, faculty, and staff from the first 25 years share from their time at Evangel?

Shared Living Experiences and Relationships

Survey data indicates the relationships developed at Evangel to be a shared experience for individuals from that time as indicated in Figure 19 above. It was mentioned in several survey responses that many faculty and staff lived in separate barracks on campus yet with the students in the early years. Participants noted that the experience of shared living space provided the foundation for deep relationships to form. One survey respondent explained,

> "Shared experiences strengthen the bonds of friendships and relationships. The friendships I developed at Evangel are the most formative and enduring part of what I took away from Evangel. The memories of life at Evangel during the era of the barracks was unique. They kind of gave us an identity caused us to be creative in inventing ways to take pride our dorm. Those kind of memories bound us together and caused to feel close to each other. I still identify as a resident of Dorm 67. It's part of who I am."

Open-ended survey responses indicated the relationship-building experiences explained the impact Evangel's culture had on the lives of the respondents. The World War II barracks were old and living in them was challenging, but most respondents look back fondly on the unique housing experience. One respondent noted, "I loved the barracks and was appreciative of the fact that Evangel did not wait for beautiful buildings to begin." On the other hand, the barracks were also mentioned as a weakness of Evangel but not as an inhibitor for those who chose to attend and remain. In fact, many respondents expressed a desire for there to still be one or two barracks on campus for posterity's sake to show the foundations from where the institution has grown.

Powerful Chapel Experiences

Another consistent shared experience included powerful spiritual experiences in the chapel services and activities during spiritual emphasis weeks. Undergirding these experiences was the spiritual leadership provided by the presidents of the time. It was often mentioned that chapel attendance was at its height when the president was speaking. Several survey responses supported this contention. One participant noted:

> My most memorable experience was seeing Dr. Kendrick, the president of the college, in our chapel services down praying with each student around the altar. He stayed until the last student finished praying. Never in a hurry. Very concerned with each student and their problems. He remembered one's name and would greet you by it.

Another survey respondent mentioned, "Dr. Ashcroft speaking in chapel [was] awesome, [he was a] wise man of God." Still another respondent added, "[We had] some awesome chapel services, especially those special services by President Robert Spence." Finally, the sentiment of what leadership meant to the students was summed up by another survey respondent who concluded, "We had Dr. Spence. What more can you say?"

Several strong terms to describe spiritual experiences were specifically mentionedby survey respondents. The term *revival* was used by respondents to describe a deep spiritual experience or event that broke the normative experience of the schedule at the time. Some participants discussed chapel services that would last longer than the allotted time. Many of them experienced spiritually transformative experiences during a dedicated week of spiritual development known as *Spiritual Emphasis Week*. This event was held near the beginning of every semester and the tradition continues to the present day. Respondents mentioned several highly spiritual events that occurred in 1963, 1974, and 1977.

Shared Challenges

Weaknesses were also shared amongst the respondents. The lack of adequate facilities during the early years was mentioned by several respondents as being a weakness. Another weakness shared by respondents included rules governing student life that were too strict, legalistic, or restrictive. One survey respondent noted a major weakness was the "legalism that has historically plagued the Pentecostal movement, which the A/G has largely come out of in recent years." For some of the participants, the emphasis on the AG tradition was too strong and off-putting. One respondent complained the influence of the AG was "too restrictive, too many rules [and the school placed] too much emphasis on AG denomination, instead of being a Christ follower, regardless of denomination."

While some respondents expressed there was a strong variety of classes offered, others felt the variety was too small. This was indicated by one participant who noted, "For a small private college, there was a good variety of courses and majors to choose from." However, another participant disagreed, "1. There was a very limited number of majors. 2. There was a very small variety of class [sic] offered." There were also some who felt the academics were too weak and others who felt they were too hard. One respondent indicated there was "not enough emphasis on academic and arts programs." Another respondent contended, "Biblical studies were so HARD and not a help for personal use and growth."

The overarching theme regarding academics that was shared by some of the participants was best described as inconsistency of the academic strength among the faculty. Most of the faculty members were beloved and did well in training students, but there were some who fell short of the academic standard students needed as part of their training.

Students' Introduction to Evangel

Survey respondents indicated they were introduced to Evangel in a variety of ways before deciding to attend. Figure 26 reveals that the most common way students were introduced to the school (outside of their parents) was through AG Publications such as the *Pentecostal Evangel* (17%).

Figure 26

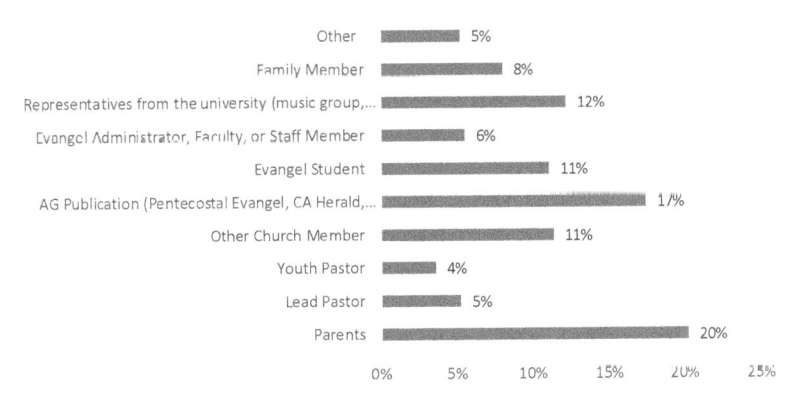

Source	%
Other	5%
Family Member	8%
Representatives from the university (music group,...)	12%
Evangel Administrator, Faculty, or Staff Member	6%
Evangel Student	11%
AG Publication (Pentecostal Evangel, CA Herald,...)	17%
Other Church Member	11%
Youth Pastor	4%
Lead Pastor	5%
Parents	20%

How did you first learn about Evangel?

Although the *Pentecostal Evangel* ceased publication in 2014, between 1955 and 1980 the weekly publication was sent to all AG churches around the country. It shared news and information related to the denomination, and Evangel had a consistent advertisement in the publication. Attention to the advertisement in the *Pentecostal Evangel* was referenced by many students through the survey and in personal interviews. One respondent summarized a common experience of student recruitment at the time:

> I had been accepted to a state university in Michigan and didn't even apply to Evangel until late May. I only knew about Evangel because of reading about it in the *Pentecostal Evangel*. I was surprised to receive a quick acceptance letter. I had very little knowledge of the college and was really surprised when I stepped foot on campus to find the old barracks buildings and only three modern buildings. However, I quickly discovered that the core of the college experience lay in the friends that I made and in the quality of the faculty, and the richness of the chapel services. I was asked to participate in a student/faculty advisory group, found opportunities for service in SCOPE, and participated in concert choir and the college band. I met my wife at Evangel and made many other lifelong friends.

A concern often mentioned is that Evangel lost a significant recruiting tool when the *Pentecostal Evangel* ceased publication. Data collected through survey and interviews for this study supports this contention. Participants mentioned they heard about Evangel through their parents' link to the publication. For example, SI3 shared:

> Life was good, and I was having the time of my life, and dad and mom said you need to go to college. So, I said okay let's go to college and dad had seen about Evangel in the *Pentecostal Evangel* and that is where I ended up.

SI2.3 also mentioned the impact of the *Pentecostal Evangel* that aligned with the parental influence on the decision to attend Evangel:

> I heard about Evangel; really my mother heard about it through the publication the *Pentecostal Evangel* and she wanted me to go to a Christian school. I had friends that were Church of God and they were trying to get me to go to Lee College in Cleveland, Tennessee and I had applications and everything ready to fill out and go there and she really encouraged me to go to Evangel because they were Assemblies and she wanted me to meet an Assemblies girl and that was primarily the reason.

Relationship-Friendly Environment

The family atmosphere and depth of relationships were one of the main talking points that spanned across the different interviews with participants. Alumni and school leader participants consistently discussed the importance of relationships they developed while at Evangel. Faculty and staff interviewees who were on campus in the early years also mentioned these characteristics as important to the school culture. LI4 noted, "On a larger scale, we were a family and we associated with one another outside of work hours." The underlying common bond among the students, faculty, and leaders centered around faith and helped create the atmosphere where many strong and lasting relationships were formed. Many interviewees discussed how they met their spouses and formed lifelong friendships while on campus. They also noted how drastically those relationships impacted their lives and livelihoods in the years that followed.

Even within the community of faith, however, a diversity of backgrounds and experiences existed. From the students' perspective, this was an important part of the Evangel experience. SI2.1 explained:

> There was almost 350 in my graduating class, and I was the only one in the whole class that was a Christian and now there is all these people and we all think together and I have all these people to be friends with and they are from all over the United States. They all had these different accents, and they were all friendly, so open and friendly. It was just amazing to see how different it was.

A review of the faculty meeting minutes reveals that a broad array of topics was discussed. The meeting minutes also illuminate that immense care was demonstrated for one another from celebrating important dates together to honoring those with significant professional accomplishments in their careers and for Evangel. As a result, deep relationships formed as evidenced in the historical documents.

Spiritual Formation and Development

The experiences shared by the interviewees supported the idea that spiritual development was highly connected to the relationships formed on campus. The strength of the relationships that were formed created an environment conducive to deep spiritual formation and development. This met the goal of the early administrators who desired to create a Pentecostal institution characterized as a "total learning environment."

Essays, articles, and speeches recovered from the archives that were written and delivered by Evangel's presidents during the first 25 years demonstrate that they made the spiritual development of students the top priority during their administrations. Their own words confirm that both the spiritual and academic development of students were preeminent goals for all three presidents.

Life-Altering Academic Experiences
When speaking of Evangel's strengths, SI9 reported, "The focus [was] on the students, to help them grow in their mission in life and not just about academics." Of course, the strength of the academics had to exist for the school to persist. The stories interviewees shared revealed life-altering experiences in the classroom. The data indicated that early faculty members were highly invested in Evangel's mission and its students, and this dedication made them highly influential on the students. When discussing faculty influence, SI2.2 reflected:

> Stan Burgess... was a history teacher and he made history come alive. I never was interested in history and ended up being a history minor. He was amazing. He would sit on his desk and rattle off dates and this battle and that battle. It was just phenomenal, and you wanted to be just like him. I was his assistant grading papers and stuff like that because of my English background.

Several similar stories were shared that involved professors from many different academic departments. Participants also noted that many professors interacted with students outside of the classroom and even invited students to their homes.

Academic Rigor
Eventually, the rigorous academics that existed in the founding years strongly contributed to the institution's ability to quickly gain regional accreditation. The school quickly gained a reputation as a noteworthy institution that was effective in

preparing students for their chosen fields. As an Evangel leader of the time, LI4 remarked:

> I think I found, for the most part, our faculty were tough academically because we always had a sense of competition with [local institutions] Drury and SMS [Southwest Missouri State] and they were looking down on us so we were bound and determined to keep our standards high. One of [our accomplishments] I think was the fact that we established ourselves early as a credible rigorous institution and during those 25 years we established ourselves [as a quality school] with our neighboring institutions and institutions around the country.

Along with quality academics, faculty, staff, and other leaders at Evangel understood the need for practicality in the type of education being delivered. LI2.2 contended:

> At the same time, it has to have a very high quality of education that catches the eye of the world, practical education. Education is not some esoteric thing that you develop and say 'Hey, I'm educated.' You are not educated until you have a practical use of that education.

Sometimes, that practicality was not immediately realized during the participants' years as students. An alumni participant reported that one professor assigned a full paper to be written every week on a different subject. The professor's students felt it was unnecessary, overzealous, and frankly, too much. Later, that alum became the commanding officer for a branch of the U.S. military and was required to write weekly reports for the President of the United States and the Joint Chiefs of Staff. At that point, he remembered his professor from Evangel and realized he had been prepared well for that position in his undergraduate years.

Historical documents serve as evidence that Evangel leaders and faculty were committed to providing a quality educational environment. Two self-study reports compiled in 1962 and 1964 and presented to the North Central Association on Accreditation also reveal the strength of academics present in the formative years of the institution. Both reports included nearly 300 pages of data and commentary to support the academic strength that was developing at Evangel

Research Sub-Question 3
The third research sub-question addressed during this study asked, "From the perspective of the faculty, staff, and alumni, what historical events during the first 25 years of Evangel University's existence shaped the foundational ethos of the institution?" Regarding the formation of the foundational ethos, there seemed to be a consistent "underdog mentality" regarding the new institution for a variety of reasons. The lack of facilities, a lack of accreditation, and a seemingly second-tier perspective of students who did not pursue vocational ministry contributed to the underdog status of the college. SI4 illustrated the point:

> At that time there was kind of, in the church that I grew up in, and more widespread than ought to have been, a bias against education, for ministers in particular. 'If you were under the anointing, you didn't need that book learning.'

This attitude of the church solidified Evangel as a different choice for many while still providing a safe, Pentecostal learning environment that was desired by students interested in other vocations. Pursuing both spiritual development and academic excellence created a unique endeavor and certainly contributed to a foundational ethos that deeply impacted the institution.

Introduction of Extracurricular Activities

As school leaders continued to build out the college experience for students, strategic extracurricular opportunities were added. A significant growth event during the first 25 years revolved around the founding of the football team. Archival data indicates how significantly enrollment grew after the football program began in 1977. However, the introduction of sports on campus became more than that. While at first glance the spiritual, academic, and extracurricular worlds may appear to be segregated endeavors, at Evangel they seemed to coalesce. For example, one survey respondent shared this story:

> There was a significant revival on campus after the founding of the football team in 1977. I saw firsthand the impact of Coach Duron and the players. There was a strong sense of hunger for God on campus and the chapel services were electric, charged with the power of God. A strong sense of expectation permeated the chapel and the entire campus.

When asked, "In your time there, what were some things that Evangel did to help foster community?", SI1 responded:

> [The] football program… There is something about everyone getting together and cheering for the same thing and sure baseball and track are great, but football is a big deal. It is the band, it's the cheer, it's the tailgating all week long. It's, what did you hear? Who is injured? What's going on? Hey, who plays? etc.

LI4, a faculty member at the time the football program began, shared what he knew about its founding:

> That was certainly a Dr. Spence loop, and he kept it pretty close to his vest up until the time that he announced it. I think that there were some moaning and groaning among

the faculty, but it turned out to be very spectacular. And to beat SMS in a football game!

For those who were on campus when it happened, Evangel beating Southwest Missouri State University's established NCAA football team in the second year of the Evangel program was considered one of the key events in the first 25 years.

Establishment of Emphasis on Vocational Calling

In the early years of Evangel, the idea that all persons have a calling to pursue was instilled as a foundational belief. Study data indicates most of the professors held the belief that the Christian calling was broader than vocational ministry or missionary work. They intentionally modeled that they were living out their calling by meeting their students' educational and spiritual needs. They often sacrificed their own career advancement and livelihood because they were pursuing something deeper. LI3, one of the earliest administrators who contributed greatly to laying this foundation, shared the story of his own experience in understanding his ministry and calling:

> [My understanding occurred] at some place along the journey, I don't remember anyone specifically addressing that all of us are called and it takes different shapes and forms and can change over time. So very early I go out to visit my pastor dad in [his home state] and we were downtown on the square in this college town, small town, 15,000 maybe, talking to two of the businessmen that he knew and he introduced me, 'This is my son...and he is teaching at our college in Springfield, Mo. He left the ministry to go to teach at the college.' So, I looked for the first opportunity to raise the topic with my dad. I knew his background, I knew what had influenced it and I said, 'Dad, I would like you to consider that I didn't leave the ministry,

just changed the kind of ministry. I am as committed to the work of the Lord now as I ever was.'

Accreditation and Establishing the Priority of Integration of Faith and Learning

With the core belief of calling embedded in the environment, there were several other significant events that impacted the development of the institution. Gaining accreditation was significant, but for the students, that was simply an external recognition of the strong experience they already had through their professors. Gaining accreditation was part of the mission from the very beginning for the leaders and administrators of the institution. The accreditation that was established early through the University of Missouri was just the beginning, but that accreditation would not carry the students pursuing degrees in Education who needed to have a fully accredited degree to directly enter the teaching profession immediately after graduation. Others who were continuing their educational pursuits in graduate programs would also be directly impacted by the institution gaining accreditation. In the lead up to becoming fully accredited in 1965, students could sense the importance and the impact it would have on Evangel, and there was significant celebration that ensued when it became official.

The participants mentioned the development of their faith being addressed through the experiences in chapel, revivals, and spiritual emphasis weeks. At the same time, faculty were naturally integrating faith and learning in the classroom, and accreditation recognized the learning aspect of that effort. Participants related that faith was supported during the classroom experience at Evangel and helped them make their faith their own. LI4 explained:

Presentation of Findings

It is not that we just have a formal prayer [in class], but it goes beyond that. It goes beyond that formality to the way a professor conducts a class and how he integrates faith and learning. That is where it takes place and I think our faculty were very good at doing that and still are.

SI4 described the impact of the classroom emphasis on integrating faith and learning:

The other thing it did for me, because I grew up in a pretty isolated area, and grew up in a church where pretty much anything you thought of as fun, was probably sin. Very conservative. And when I came to Evangel, there were kids from all over the country, west coast, east coast, Texas and there was quite a variety of backgrounds and experiences and one of the things that helped me understand and grow as a Christian was that it wasn't all about the dos and don'ts, it's about the commitment, the heart for Christ and there may be variations in how you act that out but there is not just one way and there is room for grace.

Construction of Permanent Buildings

The permanent development of the campus in terms of building projects is also a significant part of the institution's foundational ethos. In the beginning, Evangel housed students and began holding classes in World War II army hospital barracks. Interestingly, when asked about the significant experiences or events that occurred on campus or Evangel's strengths, very little is mentioned about facilities. Most responses revolve around the relationships formed and spiritual development experienced. On the other hand, each permanent building that was constructed added legitimacy to the college's programs and represented a small victory toward sustainable permanence. SI9 explained, "The top accomplishments were the new buildings. The foundation was already in place for having a quality education from a young, fledgling college, so when the first building was built, the Kendrick Library, that was a sight to behold."

Influence of External Events

In addition to the historical events that occurred on campus, there were significant global events occurring during this timeframe that contributed to the contextual foundation of education at Evangel. From the beginning, Evangel was operating within a global environment coming out of a major world war, World War 2. The atmosphere at the time contributed to the felt need for education and training for military members returning home needing new skills to enter the workforce.

Though Evangel admitted students from all ethnic backgrounds from its inception, the Civil Rights Movement was taking place as Evangel was achieving regional accreditation. Additionally, the sexual ethics and anti-authority rhetoric that characterized the 60s and 70s contributed to an understanding of the need to transcend culture for most students and families connected to Evangel. The "Jesus Revolution" largely led this effort to pursue the counter-cultural trend of the mainstream culture. It seemed as though the increase in the social upheaval increased the felt need for the Evangel experience the desire to pursue it for young people.

Research Sub-Question 4

The final research sub-question addressed by this study asked, "Which themes emerge when alumni reflect upon their respective careers and contexts?" Alumni reflected on many major experiences and events at Evangel and shared more specific insights related to their different careers. The themes that emerged from this reflection included the importance of maintaining a strong faith, the influence of shared experiences, and continuing to maintain and develop important relationships. Since Evangel served as the flagship school for the AG denomination, an additional component investigated during this study to determine Evangel's impact was the success of one of its founding missions to perpetuate the AG Pentecostal tradition among students. Denominational affiliation before and after attendance at Evangel and current denominational affiliation is addressed first. Figures 23, 24, and 25 reveal the faith and denominational journeys of the study's respondents as determined by the alumni survey.

Maintaining a Strong Faith

While many students expressed the impact the spiritual development they experienced at Evangel had on their lives, it was also a common report how that translated to maintaining a strong faith after leaving Evangel. One survey respondent reminiscing about their top memories expressed, "Rigorous integration of faith and learning in several classes anchored my Christian faith stronger than ever." The idea was commonly shared that the faith developed at Evangel wound up serving as an important foundational part of the continued faith development that continued long after leaving Evangel. Another student explained Evangel's strengths as, "Encouraging deep faith commitments as a foundation for life and not just moments of exuberant worship"

Many interview respondents would explain how the professors modeled what it meant to integrate one's faith into their callings and careers. This was echoed in survey respondents as one alumnus explained it this way, "We were challenged and taught to think critically about our beliefs, about how we could integrate our faith into our careers and the world around us." Maintaining a strong faith was instilled as being important for the individual, the community surrounding the individual, and for life in general as one respondent expressed, again, how leaders on campus modeled what it looked like as, "Coaching and guidance and examples in how to live a victorious Christian life."

Denominational Affiliation

Figure 27 reveals 93.6% of respondents considered themselves adherents to the AG prior to attending Evangel. This represents an overwhelming majority of the participants and may have contributed to the continuity of shared experiences for students during that time.

Figure 27

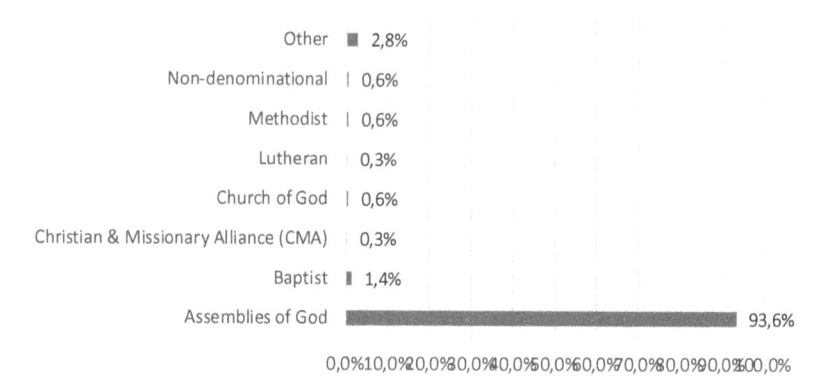

Denomination	Percentage
Other	2.8%
Non-denominational	0.6%
Methodist	0.6%
Lutheran	0.3%
Church of God	0.6%
Christian & Missionary Alliance (CMA)	0.3%
Baptist	1.4%
Assemblies of God	93.6%

Church Affiliation Prior to Evangel

Figure 28 reveals the respondents' claimed church affiliation immediately after their time at Evangel. The data indicates a significant majority (87.7%) of participants continued as adherents to the AG right after their experience at Evangel.

The percentage of those who claim the Baptist denomination affiliation doubled from 1.4% to 2.8%, and there is also the addition of Presbyterian as a standalone denomination within the "other" category. Enough individuals have identified Presbyterian as a denomination that it warranted adding the denomination to the list.

Figure 28

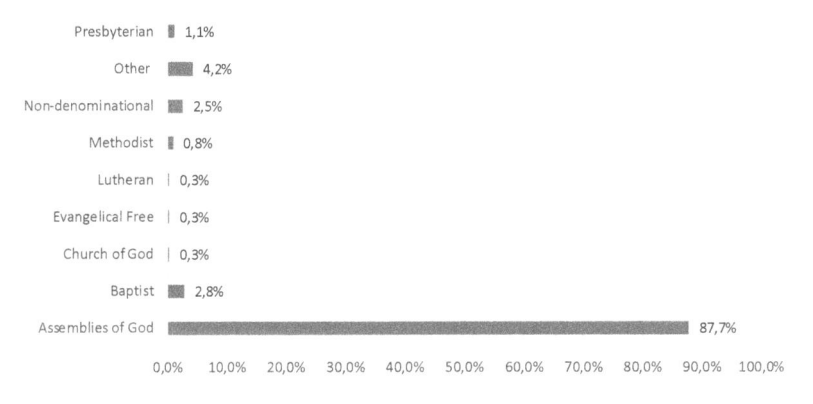

Denomination	Percentage
Presbyterian	1,1%
Other	4,2%
Non-denominational	2,5%
Methodist	0,8%
Lutheran	0,3%
Evangelical Free	0,3%
Church of God	0,3%
Baptist	2,8%
Assemblies of God	87,7%

Church Affiliation Immediately After Evangel

Figure 29 signals quite a shift in the data. Depending on when the respondents were at Evangel, this chart indicates the respondents' claim of church affiliation 43 to 68 years after their time at Evangel. At just 48.1%, the number of respondents who claimed to be affiliated with the AG at the time of this study was nearly half of what it was while they attended Evangel. Several denominations were added to the list to reflect the participants' responses in the "other" category. The second largest denomination selected is non-denominational at 21.7%. This is a significant increase from 2.5% immediately after the Evangel experience. Baptist and Presbyterian also saw a significant increase, and several other denominations were listed individually after gaining more affiliation during the time immediately after Evangel to today. These denominations are Wesleyan, Anglican, Episcopal, Nazarene, and Church of Christ.

Figure 29

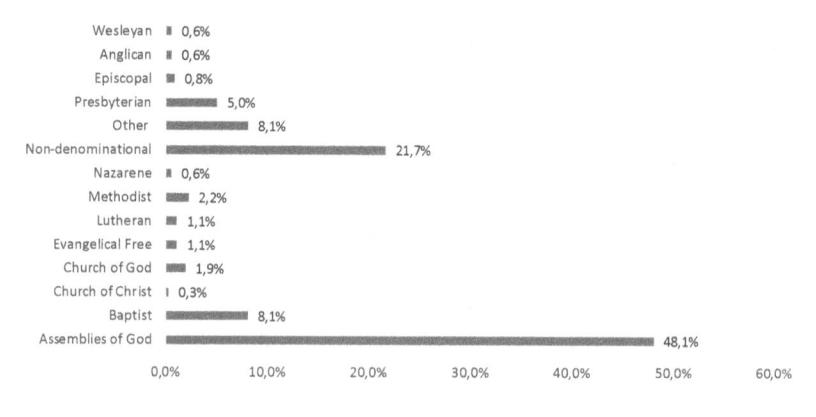

Denomination	Percentage
Wesleyan	0,6%
Anglican	0,6%
Episcopal	0,8%
Presbyterian	5,0%
Other	8,1%
Non-denominational	21,7%
Nazarene	0,6%
Methodist	2,2%
Lutheran	1,1%
Evangelical Free	1,1%
Church of God	1,9%
Church of Christ	0,3%
Baptist	8,1%
Assemblies of God	48,1%

Church Affiliation Today (2023)

Faculty and Leader Impact on Personal Spiritual Development

Study participants indicated Evangel provided a baseline for how to handle and navigate what life would bring. Many of the personal development aspects mentioned by alumni participants were modeled by the leaders on campus. These included developing a life of prayer, commitment to faith, a desire for the Holy Spirit, excellence in their field, humble and self-sacrificial leadership, and an ability to develop deep relationships. SI4 added, "It gave me a future and took me far beyond what I ever imagined what I could be and become."

Leaders on campus like President Spence provided an example of a life that was desired and emulated by those who followed including high-level administrators who served alongside him. LI4 illustrated President Spence's impact:

Of course, I think my most memorable times were with Dr. Spence. He was such a giant among men and so well respected by anyone who came in contact with him. He was dedicated, committed, honest to a fault. He had great expectations, and my attitude was I don't want to disappoint him.

A review of the oral histories in the university archives reveals leaders and administrators of the institution with a deep commitment to the same themes relayed by alumni through the survey and interviews. These historical documents show leaders with a strong commitment to their faith and prayer life, a deep conviction of the integration of faith and learning, a desire to develop the life of the mind in their students, and boldness in perpetuating the Pentecostal faith tradition.

Leaders like President Kendrick understood his assignment to care well for the spiritual lives of his students while pursuing accreditation for the institution from the outset. President Ashcroft was strongly committed to prayer and leading the students with gentleness, love, and sound Biblical principles. President Spence continued that commitment in the early years of his presidency while advancing the development of the campus and curriculum. The type of leadership exhibited by these first three presidents impacted every sector of the campus and embedded much of the ethos of Evangel that still exists today.

Influence of Shared Experience

Of those interviewed and responding to the survey, the shared experiences included the strong spiritual development that took place and the relationships that were developed. However, for those to take place, those involved had to proactively take action. The environment was certainly created for it to be easy for students to develop relationships in community while developing their faith. However, spiritual development and relationships cannot develop passively without active contributors to the formation.

A common denominator even for those students who may not have experienced strong spiritual development or even as many deep relationships was the experience of living in the barracks. Students had no choice but to experience the barracks as those austere accommodations were the only options for most of the first 25 years. In the survey, a reference to the barracks was made 55 times with many other references to army hospital and army buildings. In the personal interviews, the barracks were mentioned in every conversation. The experience of the barracks was foundational to the spiritual development, relationships, and academic learning. One respondent expressed, "I loved the barracks and was appreciative of the fact that Evangel did not wait for beautiful buildings to begin."

In some ways, the humble beginnings of the facilities of the institution contributed to the environment that focused on more of the internal development of the students as opposed to grandiose external accommodations. Fewer distractions seemed to lead to deeper development. On respondent explained it this way,

> "The chapel was smaller, more intimate. The new architecture is nice, but a chapel that is built to hold an overflow crowd for graduation can make you feel like a few golf balls bouncing around in a gymnasium the rest of the year. By necessity, we learned to look at the content rather than the wrapper. I'm not sure today's students get that culture. Being authentic in a barracks beats trying to make things look shiny on the outside."

Lifelong Relationships

The importance and impact of the relationships that were developed for students was referenced 52 times in the open-ended survey responses and in all of the personal interview discussions. One respondent explained it as a strength at Evangel when they said, "Lifetime friendships with other students were made and continue!" Another respondent mentioned it as a strength because they had "opportunities to serve and built deep friendships that endure to this day." Another respondent expressed, "The relationships I made during my time at Evangel are still precious to me today." Many others talked about the longevity of relationships that were spawned during their time at Evangel. Those relationships included fellow students, faculty leaders, and staff members.

Summary

Data was collected for this research in three different methods. Personal, one-to-one interviews with alumni and leaders of the institution during the first 25 years were reviewed. Transcriptions of these interviews were used to identify emerging themes from the stories and experiences of the interviewees. Questions that guided these interviews are listed in Appendix B. This review helped develop the appropriate questions that would become a part of the next stage of the research.

The survey was created and shared with all alumni who had an accessible email address and attended the institution from 1955 to 1980. In total, three emails were sent inviting alumni to participate in the survey. The questions used in the survey are available in Appendix D. With 387 respondents to the survey, a reasonable sample size was gained.

Historical documents such as meeting minutes, oral history transcripts, programs, personal correspondence, press releases, news articles, and other materials were utilized to shape the narrative from the institution's perspective. Important factors identified in the historical documentation included the development of permanent buildings, the importance of achieving accreditation, and the compassionate relationships the presidential leaders had with each other and those with whom they corresponded. With so much material that could be included, an effort was made to focus the review on the leadership and experiences of the presidents who lead during the timeframe of the study. This revealed key attributes that were supported by data from the interviews and surveys.

These key attributes contributed to the development of the ethos of the institution. Those attributes, such as self-sacrificial leadership, commitment to maintaining personal and communal spiritual development, the pursuit of Truth and academic excellence, the influence of shared experiences on campus, and development of lifelong relationships will be more deeply considered in Chapter 6.

CHAPTER SIX
DISCUSSION

Introduction

This study aimed to expand on Corey's (1993) research by reviewing the history and experiences of alumni, faculty, and leaders during Evangel University's first 25 years of existence from 1955 to 1980. Corey (1993) lays a foundation for understanding the genesis of Evangel and provides a historical retrospective on education within the Assemblies of God denomination, the social and cultural constructs that existed during the founding years, and decisions that were specific to Evangel. The purpose of this current study is to continue the exploration of Evangel's historical ethos by building on the strong foundation of Corey's (1993) work.

Evangel is still considered young within the context of higher education, yet an examination of its relatively short history reveals a growing legacy through the world-changing actions and influence of its alumni. For this historical review, former professors, alumni, and administrators who were present at the founding have contributed firsthand accounts of the university's early history. Their accounts are essential to produce an accurate portrayal and understanding of the early years of a denominational institution and how it persisted. These experiences accurately recorded and shared, can provide a depth of insight into the core mission and context of the university. By accurately analyzing the university's formative years, insight can be gleaned to ensure the university's mission continues to drive the decision-making of current and future leaders.

Purpose of the Study

The purpose of this study is to explore by synthesizing common themes derived from firsthand accounts of Evangel alumni, former professors, and administrators who lived the history during the period being studied into a historical narrative. The work builds on Corey's (1993) dissertation and Corey's (2005) historical narrative detailing the founding of the institution. An additional purpose of the collective narrative is to identify events, experiences, and strategies that contributed to the institutional persistence, academic preparation, and flourishing faith integration that characterized the Evangel University experience since its founding in 1955.

To narrow the focus of the study, the narrative only includes perspectives from the first 25 years (1955 – 1980) of Evangel's history. An equally important purpose of this study is to discover how the original mission of the institution was executed at Evangel within the first 25 years. The results of this investigation may help university leaders establish a vision for the future while continuing to work toward mission fulfillment. This study continues the historical narrative established through Corey's (1993) work that described the founding of Evangel. As the university ages, a growing body of historical narratives and methodologies will contribute to a consistent understanding of how the mission is being understood and executed on campus and in the lives of alumni. The hope is that the current work will establish a precedent on how to conduct future studies on the university in quarter-century increments.

Chapter 6 includes a discussion of the research findings and presents inferences and conclusions to address the research questions at the core of the study. Additionally, the interpretation of the research findings directly offers implications for practice to address the central question of the study which is, "What practices from the first twenty-five years of Evangel University can be applied to positive, successful mission fulfillment in the future?" The remaining sub-questions will also be addressed to further the discussion.

Summary of Findings

This research was conducted using one-to-one personal interviews to glean insight into alumni experiences at Evangel. Additionally, a mass survey was sent to alumni to broaden the scope of the insights gleaned. Finally, a review of historical documents produced historical data and establish the context for the participants' perspectives. The following summary provides the findings in relation to the study's research questions and the assumptions held by the researcher prior to the collection of data for the study.

The Impact of Spiritual Development on Personal and Professional Life

The first research sub-question for the study was, "How do alumni perceive the spiritual development they experienced while at Evangel University impacted their personal and professional lives?" Survey and interview participants seemed to feel the relationships they established were most influential to their spiritual development. Most significantly, they rated their relationships with professors and the school's leaders as highly influential.

The Professor as Role Model Influence

Interestingly, while chapel services and spiritual emphasis weeks were commonly expressed as being pivotal moments in the spiritual experience and development for students, the individuals who were involved were credited with having the biggest influence. Respondents rated the statement that Evangel "revealed teachers/faculty who modeled and reinforced how to grow spiritually" as the second highest factor in influencing their spiritual development. That statement is also supported by Bandura's social learning theory which credits modeling as a huge influence on learning. Presidents Kendrick and Ashcroft understood the importance of the type of faculty who were hired and took meticulous care with the process of staffing the university's classrooms with strong faith-filled role models from the very beginning. Leader interview responses concurred with the importance of careful faculty selection. L12.1 noted continuing to choose the faculty carefully is an important practice to follow to ensure Evangel continues to keep faith as its foundation. A former leader added this task falls to the leaders of the university and suggested:

> [Leaders must] choose a faculty that will do what Evangel stands for…. Have students well-grounded. What I started to say is in the smaller college, the interaction of the faculty with the students is important and you need to keep that interaction.

The Leadership/Relationship Influence

Another important finding of this study was the strength and depth of relationships. The relationships the presidents had with the staff and faculty were evident in the way they practiced such deep, impactful self-sacrificial leadership. While the presidents were held in high esteem by students, they did not have a substantial impact on the students' decisions to enroll in the school. When survey respondents were asked to rate the factors that impacted their enrollment decision, the president of the university averaged a rating that was second lowest on the list of factors. However, once the students arrived, and were able to develop a relationship with the president, this changed as is evident in the many responses shared in the survey. Many respondents indicated that the president during their time knew their names and spent time getting to know them personally. These comments represent strong anecdotal evidence of the self-sacrificial leadership displayed by these leaders in prioritizing student needs and relationships.

Sense of Unity

Many respondents to the study shared how there was a common foundational community atmosphere present on campus that helped students feel a sense of continuity in momentum. Some characterized it as feeling like everyone was moving in the same direction with their faith. Though students were in different stages of their spiritual development, they perceived that others were moving with them toward deeper faith. This experience helped develop a sense of community on campus and exemplify the strengths of a sound biblically functioning community. The sense of unity was accelerated by faculty and staff on campus and revealed how to carry out a spiritually-based calling in a professional vocation. Students learned how to take ownership of their faith and apply it to their professional contexts in their lives after Evangel.

The Importance of Shared Experiences

The second research sub-question addressed by the findings was, "What experiences do alumni, faculty, and staff from the first 25 years share from their time at Evangel?" The investigation uncovered several commonly shared experiences that made the Evangel experience uniquely powerful to the students' development. These shared experiences included how they were introduced to Evangel, their spiritual and academic development, and ultimately, the physical plant of the university and its significant impact on students.

Introduction to Evangel

The impact the weekly AG publication known as the *Pentecostal Evangel* had on students learning about Evangel cannot be overstated. Survey respondents named this publication as the second most influential factor regarding their introduction Evangel. It was assumed the publication would rate highly in the survey because of how commonly it was referenced in interviews. It was a surprise just how highly it was rated in the survey. Based on the survey, parents and the *Pentecostal Evangel* had a significant impact on leading students to Evangel. This also indicates just how many students came from families who were connected to the AG and knew about the development of Evangel through their parents.

Establishment of Faith Integration and Calling

The first assumption of the researcher prior to conducting the study was that the current emphasis on the integration of faith and learning and the discovery of vocational calling existed as part of the student experience from the beginning of the institution. Interestingly, a review of the personal interviews and mass survey responses reveals mixed feedback regarding this assumption. For example, when asked to respond to a set of statements, survey respondents provided the lowest rating to the statement, "My Evangel experience contributed to my understanding of calling." Those who were present at the institution in the early years indicated there was a sense of calling, but it was not characterized in those terms. According to interview data, an early administrator was responsible for developing that part of the ethos of the institution, and it was solidified later in the 25-year segment being studied. Alumni participants from the later years were more inclined to note that the specific terms integration of faith and learning and vocational calling were openly referenced and discussed on campus.

Spiritual and Academic Experiences

With presidents who felt the spiritual development of the students was the top priority of the Evangel experience, there was strong emphasis on creating the atmosphere for powerful spiritual experiences to take place. Chapel was a common place for these types of experiences to occur, and it was broadly stated across interviews and surveys. There were many times when alumni would share about a pivotal moment in their Evangel experience occurring often in a chapel service, residence hall, or in a classroom where the opening prayer never stopped.

Working in tandem with these spiritual experiences was the academic development students experienced. With accreditation being the focus from the beginning, students were challenged academically to equip them for their vocation and prove Evangel was deserving of being accredited. Students often shared how they came in to Evangel uncertain of what to expect and left with the ability to rise above other new entrants to the workforce because of their preparation at Evangel. The academic preparation provided the technical expertise to excel while the spiritual formation gave them the foundational self-confidence to work collaboratively and compassionately.

The Barracks Experience

Prior to the study, the researcher assumed the investigation would reveal a component of the Evangel experience that went beyond the traditional faith integration and spiritual development prevalent at other Christian higher education institutions. Though not obviously related directly to a distinctive element like spiritual development or faith integration, there was a factor that surfaced when alumni responses to both the interviews and the surveys were analyzed. That distinctive element of Evangel was the shared experience of having lived in and attended classes in the old army barracks that made up the physical plant of the early university. Though there were several permanent buildings completed during the first 25 years, the campus was still predominantly made up of old army barracks. The shared barracks experience went a step further than the shared experience of spiritual development and faith integration. Effective spiritual development and faith integration require the student to be receptive to those elements. To develop spiritual life or integrate faith into vocational calling, students must proactively and intentionally take action to instill that knowledge into their lives. Receptivity to faith integration and vocational calling as goals was not dependent on the living conditions within the barracks. After all, students had little choice but to live in the barracks. It was simply a way of life. However, the unique barracks experiences created a common bond that spanned the entire era and contributed to the unity and community that was evident in the responses to the interviews and surveys.

Given the close quarters that exemplified the living conditions in the barracks, examples of students intentionally developing their spiritual lives and integrating their faith became much more evident. These students modeled the concepts as living goals for other students who may have been less inclined to absorb them on their own. The physical space of the barracks significantly contributed to the spiritual component of the total learning environment established early on at Evangel.

The Impact of Historical Events on the Ethos of the Institution

The third research sub-question was, "From the perspective of faculty, staff, and alumni, what historical events during the first 25 years of Evangel University's existence shaped the foundational ethos of the institution?" During this period, the institution achieved regional accreditation, extracurricular activities were added, permanent buildings were erected, and society outside the university went through significant changes. The following subsections describe how the internal and external events impacted what was happening on the burgeoning campus.

Accreditation Achieved

Students who attended Evangel prior to accreditation were more interested in being part of something new. They shared that they were drawn to the novelty of an upstart institution designed to cater to those who felt a calling outside of vocational ministry. One survey respondent explained, "There was excitement at new beginnings shared amongst both faculty and students." However, achieving accreditation was significant for many students who later chose to attend Evangel. In fact, survey responses indicated accreditation held the third highest impact on the decision to attend Evangel. Besides the significance of legitimacy that was achieved through accreditation, the process and work it took to achieve accreditation greatly contributed to the foundational ethos of the institution. The underdog mentality it took to achieve accreditation relatively quickly for an institution of higher education was embedded in the DNA of the university from the beginning. This instilled a belief that the faculty, staff, and students would do whatever it took to successfully pursue accreditation, succeed in the classroom, and succeed in life after Evangel.

Extracurricular Activities

As each extracurricular activity was added to the program, the atmosphere on campus felt more like a college. Students were able to get more involved on campus as the total learning environment was developed. One survey respondent shared, "There were many ways for students to connect with each other." Activities included student clubs, organizations, intramural sports, and varsity athletics. Students did not have to wait for adequate facilities to be developed for these opportunities to become realities. The underdog mentality that helped contribute to quickly achieving accreditation helped in the development of extracurricular activities as well. The entrepreneurial spirit that characterized the early days of the college ensured leaders did not wait until the environment was perfect. It drove students, faculty, and leaders to identify needs and fill them. This led to a continually growing list of opportunities and experiences on campus. The broadening list of options for involvement also contributed to the community atmosphere on the tightly-knit campus.

Permanent Buildings Constructed

With each permanent building that was constructed, the campus deepened its roots in the community and expanded its reach into the future. While the barracks were experienced by every student who attended during the first 25 years, cohorts of students in the later years of the era enjoyed modern facilities like the library, activities center, and residence halls. These buildings continued to contribute to the growing sense of permanence of the institution while its leaders continued working through the financial challenges of modernizing the campus with unwavering faith and dogged determination.

Impact of External Events

Much like today, there was no shortage of significant global events that were impacting and shaping culture during the early development of Evangel. External events like the Vietnam War, the Civil Rights Movement, the Jesus Revolution, the Flash Crash of 1962, the Fuel Crisis of the 70s, the JFK assassination, the Beatles, the Kent State massacre, and Title IX were just a few of the deeply impactful events which occurred, and they all had an impact on the culture at large and life on a college campus. Because of the strength of the total learning environment that existed on campus and the deep relationships formed amongst the students and faculty, many students felt insulated from these types of external events and the overall environment that was shaping the external culture. However, these factors still impacted the economics and operations of the institution. Students may have been unencumbered, but financial conditions externally often impacted the institution's ability to fund building projects in different ways. Additionally, there was a constant focus and concern by the administration of the increasing liberalization of the culture and how Evangel would fare in going against it. The expressions of "free love" in the 60s and the anti-authority culture of the 70s contributed to the contexts from which students were arriving on campus at Evangel. Reframing and reshaping the worldview of incoming students was an important part of the work faculty felt they needed to accomplish. However, with most students coming from a strict AG and Pentecostal background, they were often more insulated from these external factors than students at other institutions.

Impact of Evangel Experience on Alumni Careers and Contexts

The final research sub-question asked, "Which themes emerge when alumni reflect upon their respective careers and contexts?" There are several core elements to the themes which emerged as alumni were interviewed and surveyed. These themes include the importance of maintaining and developing faith, establishing and cherishing lifelong relationships, and community and shared experiences.

Discussion

Maintaining and Development Faith

As they reflected on their Evangel experiences, many alumni indicated Evangel helped them make their faith their own. Although many grew up in Christian contexts, it wasn't until their experience at Evangel that they took ownership of their faith development. One survey respondent characterized the experience at Evangel as helping him become a "defender of his faith."

For most respondents, the importance of their Evangel experience begins and ends in this area. They noted that a deeply developed faith was the foundation from which their other life successes were achieved. Several alumni attributed this level of faith development as having begun during their time at Evangel even through more than 93% of students came from strong AG backgrounds.

Lifelong Relationships

If faith is the root providing an anchor for alumni in the midst of life's challenges, then relationships are the trunk from which all other meaningful experiences have grown. There is seemingly no end to how deeply these relationships have impacted interviewees and survey respondents. Relationships were developed with faculty, staff, and fellow students, and all made a significant impact. Many of these relationships are still intact and flourishing. Often, tears formed for interviewees when trying to accurately depict how important these relationships were and still are to them.

Community and Shared Experiences

Flowing out of the strong spiritual development and deeply held relationships that were developed is the sense of community which was experienced and remembered by alumni, faculty, and staff. Undergirding the development of relationships and community was the shared experience of doing life in the barracks. While reflecting on their lives, a reference to the impact of living in the barracks was commonly used in interviews and survey responses. The barracks could be considered the soil providing a rich context for spiritual, intellectual, and relational development to take place.

Discussion of Major Themes

Several major themes emerged from the data collected and analyzed during this study. Personal interviews, survey responses, and inspection of historical documents reveal significant evidence of self-sacrificial leadership, the importance and impact of shared experiences, founding mission fulfillment, and political awareness. The following subsections describe the major themes in detail and connect the findings of this study to the current literature.

Self-Sacrificial Leadership

The origins of theories related to self-sacrificial leadership were not solidified until the very end of the timeframe being studied. The writings of Burns (1978) and Bass (1985) popularized the theory of self-sacrificial leadership. Matteson and Irving (2006) indicated that these theorists believed the self-sacrifice of leaders was a tool used to motivate followers. Choi and Mai-Dalton (1999) agreed and found that followers' "attributions of charisma and the charismatic effects of leader behaviors on followers will be significantly stronger when the leader exhibits self-sacrificial behaviors than when the leader does not exhibit such behaviors" (p. 401). Their findings were reflected in the responses of this study's participants as they discussed the influence of the three presidents who served during the first 25 years of Evangel's existence.

Self-sacrificial leadership exemplified the biblical principles upon which the institution was attempting to set as its founding anchor. Presidents Klaude Kendrick, J. Robert Ashcroft, and Robert Spence showed tangible examples of self-sacrificial leadership and endeared themselves to their followers. According to the study's participants, they modeled behavior that was reflected in the attitudes and behaviors of the students, staff, and faculty of the college. Faculty sacrificed their own careers and financial well-being to join this upstart higher education institution. Student sacrificed their own comfort to live in the barracks, and some even sacrificed a guarantee of future employment by attending an unaccredited institution. The self-sacrificial leadership tendencies of the presidents of that time certainly influenced the leadership tendencies of faculty and staff, which then influenced students who attended.

Shared Experiences

One of the endeavors of this study is to identify aspects of the first 25 years that contributed to Evangel's early success and can be included in future plans to continue the school's legacy. Specific events and shared experiences impacted large numbers of students during that time. On the surface, the shared experiences may not be very distinctive compared to other private, Christian universities. The development of strong relationships, strong chapel experiences, spiritual development, and the integration of faith and learning are all discussed on other campuses. A major finding of this study is that the experience of living and learning in the crude and uncomfortable student housing provided by converted army barracks was a significant shared experience. The close contact and intimate quarters of the barracks deeply impacted the developing ethos and sense of unity among the early community of students, faculty, and staff. Student dorm rooms were small, offices were small, and the hallways, which ran from one end of the campus to the other in a grid-like fashion were narrow and small.

The barracks contributed to the creation of the total learning environment which was a major focus of the administration. They also created the setting for the relationships that were developed, the modeling which took place, the faith and spiritual beliefs that were development, and the faith and learning which was integrated. The shared experience of the barracks facilitated the continuity and the sense that everyone involved was moving in the same direction.

Founding Mission Fulfilled

Corey (1993) shared that one of the founding missions of the institution was to perpetuate the Assemblies of God denomination. Data gathered from the alumni survey do not provide a definitive answer regarding whether the institution achieved that mission in the first 25 years, however notable trends are illuminated. The church affiliation prior to Evangel shows that 93.6% of students were affiliated with the AG. Immediately following the experience in the total learning environment at Evangel, 87.7% indicated they were still affiliated with the AG. This data shows a remarkably high retention rate for individuals within the denomination. When asked what affiliation they had as this study was being completed, only 48.1% indicated still being affiliated with the AG. A large majority of individuals seem to have remained in the AG immediately after their experience at Evangel. Reasons for the noted decline in AG affiliation reported in the present day were not addressed in this study.

Interestingly, data collected indicated that non-denominational affiliation increased exponentially from 2.5% before alumni attended Evangel to 21.7% in the present day. A current trend within the AG denomination is to drop Assembly of God as part of the church name. While the doctrine and beliefs of the leaders within the church may remain unchanged, many attendees and members may lose their connection to and understanding of the AG denomination. The data collected through the surveys is self-reported, and it could be that because of a possible name change, the respondents see their church as non-denominational. However, this inference was not addressed in the study's data collection.

Political Awareness

It has been well-documented how critical the relationship denominational and institutional leaders had with political leaders was. From establishing the campus on which Evangel was founded to gaining the coveted accreditation, political awareness was key. It must also be noted what was happening politically off campus in the early years. From different wars impacting college-age students to the founding of organizations like the National Association of Evangelicals, of which the AG was a founding member, these external factors impacted the political atmosphere surrounding the institution.

There were many instances in the historical documentation that showed deep concerns relative to the increasing "liberalization" of education and culture. This was the other side of the challenge for the early leaders in getting the institution founded. Not only did they desire to perpetuate the AG tradition for those apathetic to higher education, but they desired to safeguard the young people in a Pentecostal total learning environment for those who were supportive of higher education.

Additionally, the organization's political acumen was key to the founding of the institution and served as the key to its persistence. The tightrope was walked throughout the first 25 years as there continued to be naysayers and doubters within the fellowship who were leery of the need for a liberal arts institution like Evangel.

Implications for Practice

There are several key takeaways that can be gleaned from the data collected through this research. These are the elements the leadership of the institution might consider when applying past successes to future plans. Several implications for practice include continuing to exemplify true self-sacrificial leadership, establishing and supporting new and unifying shared experiences, continuing to fulfill the founding mission, and maintaining political awareness.

Continue True Self-Sacrificial Leadership

For current and future institutional leaders, it is important to understand the impact self-sacrifice may have on exuding charisma, deepening the commitment of followers, and increasing the reciprocation of that self-sacrifice by alumni and donors when needed to support the continuation of institutional initiatives. In the context of a setting like Evangel, where biblical principles are overtly discussed and encouraged, self-sacrificial behaviors from leaders must be genuine and authentic. Fabricated displays of self-sacrifice undermine the enduring effectiveness of any leader attempting to increase follower engagement.

While understanding self-sacrifice took the form of a lower salary and greater time commitment to serve the students and the mission of the university, this is not necessarily something that should continue. Faculty and staff should be compensated in accordance with expectations of the roles they execute in making sure Evangel maintains its reputation for excellence in academics. Study participants mentioned that highly qualified faculty members took lower salaries to teach at Evangel than they would have at other institutions. While this may have contributed to the early high-quality educational experiences, the data did not clearly indicate that salary sacrifice by faculty was a model alumni chose to emulate. However, it should be noted that the self-sacrifice of additional time spent by faculty and school leaders in building relationships and mentoring students was demonstrated in the data as being significant to the student experience and continuing ethos of the institution.

Examples of noticeable ways to continue to exhibit sacrificial leadership are attending student events such as athletic competitions, music and theater performances, organized social events, and student variety shows. Additionally, being present in the chapel services to pray with and speak to students is recommended to continue the leader/student connections and sense of caring exhibited at Evangel from the beginning. These examples of self-sacrifice were commonly referenced by students as having a meaningful impact on them as they witnessed the leadership of the institution investing in students with their time and presence.

Support New and Unifying Shared Experiences

The barracks are now gone from the Evangel University campus. They were torn down to modernize the campus. While the campus has been significantly modernized, the shared barracks experience and its influence on the unity of early students, faculty, and staff are gone. To move into the future, the question must be asked, "What shared experiences exist across the entire institutional community?" Strong relationships are still being formed, spiritual development is still a major focus of the institution, and the understanding of calling and integration of faith and learning are discussed in much more proactive terms. The impact of not having a shared experience like the barracks may only be discerned over time when future research is conducted. However, leaders of the institution can begin looking for other opportunities to integrate a unique shared experience that would contribute to creating the desired learning environment.

One shared experience that can be amplified and expanded to touch every student could involve global missions and service trips. Currently, students are invited to participate in missions and service trips around the world, but it is possible to avoid global travel in favor of staying domestic or utilizing a previous experience. The possibility of using these missions and service trips as the new barracks-styled, shared experience was supported by the survey and interview responses during this study. Respondents noted the importance of experiences traveling with groups from the institution that built their sense of belonging and community. The groups included music groups, orchestral groups, summer camp groups, and athletic teams.

Trips tend to bond people together in deep and unique ways. Making these trip experiences a ubiquitous experience for Evangel students would function similarly to the barracks. Trips can include students with diverse backgrounds and majors. Future trips could even span different programs and include traditional undergraduate students, adult off-campus students, online students, graduate students, doctoral students, and seminary students. In the first 25 years, only on-campus residential students would have the shared experience of the barracks. Global missions and service trips could engage all students in a shared experience.

Currently, there are many students who participate in global missions and service trips. However, they participate at their own cost or fundraising effort, and it is not mandatory to go on a global trip. For that reason, the experiences do not represent shared and unifying experiences. To address this, the institution can make service trips a mandatory experience across all sectors of the student body. By finding ways to also cover the cost for students, the financial barrier to participation would be removed. Denominational and donor support could be pursued by university leadership to facilitate this as a cross-campus experience. Making this type of experience one that is mandatory across the student experience would also align with the denominational mission to evangelize the world with the gospel. The Assemblies of God has one of the most robust and sophisticated missions programs in the world. Inviting every student at the flagship liberal arts institution and national seminary for the denomination to participate in missions and service experiences that span academic departments would exemplify the founding ethos that all are called to utilize their strengths and gifts to advance the Kingdom of God globally.

Continued Fulfillment of Founding Mission

The AG denomination and the institution now have a data point which may indicate that one aspect of the founding mission of Evangel was successfully achieved, to perpetuate the Pentecostal traditions of the Assemblies of God. When placed within the context of how many individuals leave the faith when attending college, the retention in the denomination demonstrated by data from this study reveals a major success. The statistics for students who leave the faith during or after college are alarming. There is no shortage of reports or surveys that attempt to quantify the dropout rate of church attendees who reach college age. In a 2007 study, Lifeway research found that 70% of church attendees had stopped attending church at some point during their college years (*Reasons*, 2007). Barna Group researchers found that young adult dropout rates in 2011 were 59% and increased to 64% in 2019 (*Church Dropouts*, n.d.) These different studies ask different questions, but the result is an indication that a large majority of young people leave the church during their college years. Evangel fulfilled its mission to keep those individuals in church during the first 25 years of existence by keeping more than 87% of them in the AG immediately after their time at Evangel.

To continue fulfilling this part of the mission, the relationship between the denomination and institution must remain strong, and increased assistance in promotion and awareness of Evangel at the denominational level must be improved. The denomination produced the *Pentecostal Evangel* publication which was so important to helping students learn more about Evangel. Without that magazine, the denomination must explore other methods in helping promote the institution and seminary in modern ways. Without the support of the denomination, fulfilling this aspect of the founding mission to perpetuate the Pentecostal traditions of the denomination will be a challenge.

Maintain Positive Political Alliances

The relationship between Christian organizations and political entities has changed over the years regarding government politics. The landscape feels more intense and less collaborative for institutions like Evangel. Leaders of Christian institutions express they feel under attack by many government and political entities. Given the current context of the institution in a predominantly conservative region and state, it would be good practice to maintain strong relationships with the relevant political leaders who represent the district and region of the institution.

Positive political relationships are key to the future success of the institution. The historical data of the study gave multiple examples of the importance these strong relationships with political leaders had on the rise of the institution in the first 25 years. Positive political alliances facilitated acquiring the property for the campus. It was also these types of positive relationships that contributed to gaining accreditation quickly and receiving government funding for student financial aid and campus development.

Additionally, continuing to exist less than one mile from the national denominational headquarters presents many opportunities and some unique challenges. Navigating the organizational politics of the many different stakeholders within the fellowship is key to the sustained longevity of the institution. The relational development and political acumen of the leaders of the institution expressed in the historical narrative provide a blueprint for future leaders on how to navigate relationships within the denomination. Leaders with an understanding of the historical context of the institution as well as the context of the denomination will be integral to its future growth.

Limitations of the Study

In this section, the limitations to the study are addressed. First, this is a historical analysis of a single university within the private, Christian higher education context in the midwestern United States. The unique history of this institution does not match the history of other institutions, even those within the same denomination. As such, this research may not be replicable, nor the findings of this study be applicable to other institutions.

The second limitation has to do with the reach of the invitations to participate in the surveys that were sent. Evangel maintains a comprehensive database of alumni contact information which is only as accurate as the updates provided by alumni. Of the alumni and email addresses that were accessible 387 responded and completed to the survey. While it is a 24% response rate to the requests for survey participation, it is only 6.2% of the total alumni from the timeframe being studied.

Third, time limited the ability to collect more personal interviews. Not only was time a factor because of the completion of the study, but it was also a factor because of the leaders and individuals who had passed away before an interview could be conducted. There was one key alumnus of the institution who became a leader on campus and also became the leader of the entire denomination who passed away the week the interview was scheduled to be completed.

Fourth, the researcher is an undergraduate and graduate alumnus of the institution being studied. The researcher also works for the institution in a leadership position, is an adjunct faculty member, and is also completing this research as part of a doctoral program at the institution. While steps were taken to mitigate bias in data collection, the researcher's association with the university may impact the interpretation of data and inferences drawn from the study's results.

Recommendations for Future Research

There are many opportunities to advance this research in important ways. Chapter 4 attempted to provide a high-level overview and historical narrative of the first 25 years of the institution. There are key points within that history and beyond which deserve deeper consideration and research. Ideas for building on this study for future research areas include:

- A Longitudinal Analysis of the Change in Denominational Affiliation Over Time
- The Impact of the Spiritual Experiences, Moves of God, and Revivals
- The Impact of Lifelong Relationships on Career Success, Well-Being, and Mental Health
- A Historical Narrative and Student Experience Analysis of the Second Twenty-Five Years of Evangel University (1981-2005)

A Longitudinal Analysis of the Change in Denominational Affiliation Over Time

A denominational analysis might be conducted to identify the reasons and rationale for the significant drop in denominational affiliation from immediately after student experience at Evangel to the present time of this study. This may assist denominational leaders in addressing any issues that contributed to the drastic drop in affiliation and better sustain the denomination in the future. Subsequently, it may also be appropriate to do a more targeted analysis of the alumni in this study and their perceptions of the AG and the Church at large. Perhaps this targeted approach for this same demographic would produce more responses and a higher validity and reliability rate. Future research could be guided by the following questions:

- What are the alumni perceptions which contributed to any denominational affiliation changes from the time they attended Evangel to today?
- What is the denominational retention rate for alumni of AG institutions at large?

The Impact of the Spiritual Experiences, Moves of God, and Revivals

There were many different revivals mentioned in the open-ended questions of the survey and in the personal interviews. In addition to revivals, there were many significant spiritual experiences that were referenced. These events deserve further exploration to better understand the experiences of the participants and the contexts within which these experiences occurred. Research in this area might better identify events that were more common and widespread to collect similarities and patterns that were

present. Research questions related to this study would be guided by questions like:
- How do alumni, faculty, and staff characterize the different spiritual experiences which occurred during the first 25 years?
- What were the common shared characteristics, contexts, and timing of these spiritual experiences?

The Impact of Lifelong Relationships on Career Success, Wellbeing, and Mental Health

The importance of relationships was mentioned so ubiquitously throughout the research it would be appropriate to explore the impact those relationships had over time. A deeper analysis could be done to see if there is a tangible difference in the different areas of life success for alumni from the time period compared to the general population. Questions that might guide this research could be:
- What impact did relationships from the Evangel experience have on career success over time?
- Are marriage relationship success rates higher for Evangel alumni than the general public?
- Did the relationships developed at Evangel contribute to improved mental health for its alumni?

A Historical Narrative and Student Experience Analysis of the Second Twenty-Five Years of Evangel University (1981-2005)

Most notably, a similar study to this should be conducted for the next set of 25 years of existence for the university. This would produce a new set of data and findings for the next group of alumni. This research should be conducted after the similar amount of time has passed as this study. The central question for that research could be similar to the central question for this research such as:

- What practices from the second twenty-five years (1981-2005) of Evangel University can be applied to positive, successful mission fulfillment in the future?

For consistency with this research in terms of how many years have passed since the time period being studied, this research could be conducted around the years 2045-2050. However, interviews of key alumni and administrators should be compiled continually.

Summary

This study set out to collect a variety of data through personal interviews, mass surveys, and historical documents to tell a story and identify successful mechanisms for a startup university in the midwestern United States. The overarching goal has been to identify what worked well in the first 25 years, and how can it be applied to the future of the institution. The findings presented in this research may only be applicable to this institution. However, the model of conducting this research could be utilized in a variety of university settings. The findings of this research are relevant, and the implications are achievable.

The data revealed several key areas that contributed to the successful experience alumni expressed in interviews and surveys. A focus on the spiritual development and faith integration grounded students in their faith and prepared them for success in life after Evangel. The relationships formed at Evangel provided a network of support that sustained many alumni in the years since their time at Evangel. The shared experience of living in the barracks contributed to a sense of unity that pervaded the campus in the classroom and in extracurricular activities. Events on campus and around the world created an atmosphere that helped students feel a sense of community as they moved in the same direction towards deeper faith and vocational preparation.

Major themes revealed in this study included the importance of self-sacrificial leadership, the power of shared experiences, the fulfillment of the founding mission, and the importance of political awareness. These themes lay the groundwork in understanding the positive aspects of the first 25 years that contributed to the institution's success. They also will assist future leaders in understanding the importance of applying them to current contexts in modern and relevant ways to build on the strong foundation that was laid. The pipelines and platforms may change over time, but the purpose remains the same.

Future research will enhance the findings of this research and contribute to a deeper understanding of how the Evangel experience can continue shaping the lives of students, faculty, and staff. No matter the position, title, or job, the alumni from the first 25 years of the institution had a common set of shared experiences led by self-sacrificial leaders who changed the course of a denomination and impacted the world.

References

About the AG. (n.d.). Retrieved July 22, 2022, from https://ag.org/About/About-the-AG

[Articles of Agreement of Evangel College of the Assemblies of God]. (1955, August 22). Evangel University Archives, Betty Chase Archive Rooms, Accreditation Self-Study 1962, Springfield, MO, United States.

Ashcroft, J. R. (1945, February 6). [Letter to Ralph Riggs]. Evangel University Archives, Betty Chase Archive Rooms, J. Robert Ashcroft files, Springfield, MO, United States.

Ashcroft, J. R. (1954, September 11). [Letter to Klaude Kendrick]. Evangel University Archives, Betty Chase Archive Rooms, J. Robert Ashcroft files and correspondence, Springfield, MO, United States.

Ashcroft, J. R. (1958, September 3). [Joint Opening Address]. Evangel University Archives, Betty Chase Archive Rooms, J. Robert Ashcroft files, Springfield, MO, United States.

Ashcroft, J. R. (1963, June 13). [Letter to Robert H. Spence]. Evangel University Archives, Betty Chase Archive Rooms, J. Robert Ashcroft files, Springfield, MO, United States.

Ashcroft, J. R. (1973, August 1). [Letter to Executive Presbytery]. Evangel University Archives, Betty Chase Archive Rooms, J. Robert Ashcroft files, Springfield, MO, United States.

Ashcroft, J. R. (1973, August 15). [Letter to General Presbytery]. Evangel University Archives, Betty Chase Archive Rooms, J. Robert Ashcroft files, Springfield, MO, United States.

Ashcroft, J. R. (1973, September 7). [Letter to Thomas Zimmerman]. Evangel University Archives, Betty Chase Archive Rooms, J. Robert Ashcroft files, Springfield, MO, United States.

Ashcroft, J. R. (1974, April 3). [Memo to Robert H. Spence and General Council Leadership]. Evangel University Archives, Betty Chase Archive Rooms, J. Robert Ashcroft files, Springfield, MO, United States.

Ashcroft, J. R. (1988, March 24). Interview by Betty Chase [Transcript]. Evangel University Archives, Betty Chase Archive Rooms, Barry Corey Files, Springfield, MO, United States.

Ashcroft, J. R. (1988, April 19). Interview by Betty Chase [Transcript]. Evangel University Archives, Betty Chase Archive Rooms, Barry Corey Files, Springfield, MO, United States.

Assemblies of God 16 Fundamental Truths. (n.d.). Retrieved July 21, 2022, from https://ag.org/Beliefs/Statement-of-Fundamental-Truths

Bandura, A. (1971). *Bandura_SocialLearningTheory.pdf.* http://www.asecib.ase.ro/mps/Bandura_SocialLearningTheory.pdf

Bass, B. (1985). *Leadership and performance beyond expectations.* Free Press.

Bolman, L., & Deal, T. (2013). *Reframing Organizations* (Fifth). Jossey-Bass.

Burns, J. M. (2010). *Leadership* (Evangel James River Library Circulation; First Harper Perennial Political Classics edition.). HarperPerennial.

Burtchaell, J. T. (1998). *The dying of the light: The disengagement of colleges and universities from their Christian churches* (Evangel Kendrick General Circulation). W.B. Eerdmans Pub. Co.

CCCU. (2011). *CCCU report of the task force of spiritual formation in Christian higher education.*

Chase, B. (1990, July 27). [Letter to J. Robert Ashcroft]. Evangel University Archives, Betty Chase Archive Rooms, J. Robert Ashcroft files, Springfield, MO, United States.

Church Dropouts Have Risen to 64%—But What About Those Who Stay? (n.d.). Barna Group. Retrieved February 23, 2023, from https://www.barna.com/research/resilient-disciples/

[College Day Giving report]. (1957, Summer). Evangel University Archives, Betty Chase Archive Rooms, J. Robert Ashcroft files. Springfield, MO, United States.

Corey, B. H. (1993). *Pentecostalism and the collegiate institution: A study in the decision to found Evangel College* (Evangel Kendrick General Circulation). University Microfilms international. http://0-search.ebscohost.com.swan.searchmobius.org/login.aspx?direct=true&db=cat07720a&AN=eul.b3226228&site=eds-live

Creswell, J. W. (2014). *Research Design: Qualitative, Quantitative, and Mixed Methods Approaches* (4th ed.). Sage Publications.

Crider, A. L., & Crider, J. R. (2020a). SPANNING THE PEDAGOGICAL DIVIDE: A Theological Model Connecting Content and Competency. *Southwestern Journal of Theology, 63*(1), 33–51.

Crider, A. L., & Crider, J. R. (2020b). SPANNING THE PEDAGOGICAL DIVIDE: A Theological Model Connecting Content and Competency. *Southwestern Journal of Theology, 63*(1), 33–51.

Cross, C. (2022). *Registrar's Report Fall 2022* (pp. 1–23). Evangel University.

Davis, C. (2018). Strategic Indicators of Mission Fulfillment at Assemblies of God Colleges: Reaching Consensus on Faith Integration and Spiritual Formation. *Christian Higher Education, 17*(4), 250–264. https://doi.org/10.1080/15363759.2018.1440661

Davis, R. H. (1962, October 4). [Letter to J. Robert Ashcroft]. Evangel University Archives, Betty Chase Archive Rooms, J. Robert Ashcroft files, Springfield, MO, United States.

[Education Department Survey]. (1957, Spring). "Attitudes of Assemblies of God High School Students". Evangel University Archives, Betty Chase Archive Rooms, J. Robert Ashcroft files. Springfield, MO, United States.

Evangel College Opens with 87 Students Enrolled. (1955, October 30). *The Pentecostal Evangel*, 6.

[Faculty Meeting Minutes]. (1955, September 9). Evangel University Archives, Betty

Chase Archive Rooms, Faculty Meeting Minutes Binder, Springfield, MO, United States.

References

[Faculty Meeting Minutes]. (1955, November 11). Evangel University Archives, Betty Chase Archive Rooms, Faculty Meeting Minutes Binder, Springfield, MO, United States.

[Faculty Meeting Minutes]. (1956, January 17). Evangel University Archives, Betty Chase Archive Rooms, Faculty Meeting Minutes Binder, Springfield, MO, United States.

[Faculty Meeting Minutes]. (1958, April 1). Evangel University Archives, Betty Chase Archive Rooms, Faculty Meeting Minutes Binder, Springfield, MO, United States.

[Faculty Meeting Minutes]. (1973, March 8). Evangel University Archives, Betty Chase Archive Rooms, J. Robert Ashcroft Files, Springfield, MO, United States.

[Faculty Meeting Minutes]. (1973, April 12). Evangel University Archives, Betty Chase Archive Rooms, J. Robert Ashcroft Files, Springfield, MO, United States.

[Faculty Meeting Minutes]. (1974, January 8). Evangel University Archives, Betty Chase Archive Rooms, Robert H. Spence files, Springfield, MO, United States.

Falk, T., May 5, W. E., & 2020. (2020, May 5). Private colleges on life support. *Wisconsin Examiner*. https://wisconsinexaminer.com/2020/05/05/private-colleges-on-life-support/

Frey, T. (2013, July 5). By 2030 over 50 Percent of Colleges will Collapse. *Futurist Speaker*. https://futuristspeaker.com/business-trends/by-2030-over-50-of-colleges-will-collapse/

[General Presbytery Report]. (1974, August 20). Evangel University Archives, Betty Chase Archive Rooms, Robert H. Spence files. Springfield, MO, United States.

Glanzer, P. L. (Perry L., Cockle, T. F., Graber, B., Jeong, E., & Robinson, J. A. (2019). Are Nondenominational Colleges More Liberal Than Denominational Colleges?: A Comparison of Faculty Religious Identity, Beliefs, Attitudes, and Actions. *Christian Higher Education, 18*(3), 207–223. https://doi.org/10.1080/15363759.2018.1517620

Hammond, M. D. (2019). Christian Higher Education in the United States: The Crisis of Evangelical Identity. *Christian Higher Education, 18*(1–2), 3–15. https://doi.org/10.1080/15363759.2018.1554352

Ho, L., & Limpaecher, A. (n.d.). *The Practical Guide to Grounded Theory*. Delve. Retrieved June 18, 2022, from https://delvetool.com/groundedtheory

Horn, M. B. (2018). *Will Half Of All Colleges Really Close In The Next Decade?* Forbes. https://www.forbes.com/sites/michaelhorn/2018/12/13/will-half-of-all-colleges-really-close-in-the-next-decade/

Horton, R. (2017). *Handbook of Christian Education | BJU Press*. https://www.bjupress.com/product/506501

Chase Archive Rooms, Robert H. Spence files. Springfield, MO, United States.

[Important Dates]. (Unknown Date). Evangel University Archives, Betty Chase Archive Rooms, Springfield, MO, United States.

[Inauguration Address]. (1974, December 11). Evangel University Archives, Betty Chase Archive Rooms, Robert H. Spence files. Springfield, MO, United States.

References

[Inauguration Program]. (1958, September 4). Evangel University Archives, Betty Chase Archive Rooms, J. Robert Ashcroft files. Springfield, MO, United States.

[Inauguration Program]. (1974). Evangel University Archives, Betty Chase Archive Rooms, Robert H. Spence files. Springfield, MO, United States.

Kaak, P. (2016a). Academic Faith Integration: Introduction to a New Section Within Christian Higher Education. *Christian Higher Education*, *15*(4), 189–199. https://doi.org/10.1080/15363759.2016.1187988

Kaak, P. (2016b). Academic Faith Integration: Introduction to a New Section Within *Christian Higher Education*. *Christian Higher Education*, *15*(4), 189–199. https://doi.org/10.1080/15363759.2016.1187988

Kendrick, K. (Unknown Date). Interview by Larry Nelson [Transcript]. Evangel University Archives, Betty Chase Archive Rooms, Klaude Kendrick Files, Springfield, MO, United States.

Kendrick, K. (1955). *Evangel College & Higher Education.* [Speech delivered to the Springfield Chamber of Commerce]. Evangel University Archives, Betty Chase Archive Rooms, Klaude Kendrick box, Springfield, MO, United States.

Kendrick, K. (1963, March 15). [Klaude Kendrick Oral History]. Evangel University Archives, Betty Chase Archive Rooms, Klaude Kendrick Files, Springfield, MO, United States.

Kendrick, K. (1980, April 30). Interview by L. Nelson [Transcript]. Evangel University Archives, Betty Chase Archive Rooms, Larry Nelson Files, Springfield, MO, United States.

Logsdon, P. K. (2018, February). [Campus Development History]. Evangel University, University Advancement Files, Alumni Engagement Files, Springfield, MO, United States.

Lederman, D. (2017, April 28). *Clay Christensen, Doubling Down*. Inside Higher Ed. https://www.insidehighered.com/digital-learning/article/2017/04/28/clay-christensen-sticks-predictions-massive-college-closures

Lederman, D. (2021, August 2). *The Number of Colleges Continues to Shrink*. Inside Higher Ed. https://www.insidehighered.com/news/2021/08/02/number-colleges-shrinks-again-including-publics-and-private-nonprofits

Lester, S. (1999). *An introduction to phenomenological research.*

Liu, C. H., & Matthews, R. (2005). Vygotsky's Philosophy: Constructivism and Its Criticisms Examined. *International Education Journal*, *6*(3), 386–399.

Matteson, J. A., & Irving, J. A. (n.d.). *Servant versus Self-Sacrificial Leadership: A Behavioral Comparison of Two Follow-Oriented Leadership Theories*.

Mcleod, S. (2018). *Jean Piaget's Theory of Cognitive Development*. 16.

[Notes from Klaude Kendrick]. (1988, July). Evangel University Archives, Betty Chase Archive Rooms, Klaude Kendrick files (Box WR-J3-3-6-#6), Springfield, MO, United States.

Otto, P., & Harrington, M. E. (2016). Spiritual Formation Within Christian Higher Education. *Christian Higher Education*, *15*(5), 252–262. https://doi.org/10.1080/15363759.2016.1208594

References

Pattillo, M. (1955, July 13). [Letter to Ralph Riggs]. Evangel University Archives, Betty Chase Archive Rooms, Klaude Kendrick files, Springfield, MO, United States.

Piaget, J. (1981). *The psychology of intelligence: Jean Piaget* (Evangel AGTS General Circulation). Littlefield, Adams.

Piaget, J. (2003). PART I: Cognitive Development in Children: Piaget: Development and Learning. *Journal of Research in Science Teaching, 40*(Suppl), S8–S18.

Presidency of Central Bible Institute and Evangel College to be Separated July 1963. (1963, January 13). *The Pentecostal Evangel*, 28.

Reasons 18- to 22-Year-Olds Drop Out of Church. (2007, August 7). Lifeway Research. Retrieved February 23, 2023, from https://research.lifeway.com/2007/08/07/reasons-18-to-22-year-olds-drop-out-of-church/

[Recommended Placement Services]. (1958, March 12). Evangel University Archives, Betty Chase Archive Rooms, Placement Filing Drawer, Springfield, MO, United States.

Riggs, R. M. (1958, September 4). [Presidential Charge to J. Robert Ashcroft]. Evangel University Archives, Betty Chase Archive Rooms, J. Robert Ashcroft files. Springfield, MO, United States.

Riggs, R. M. (1969, October 6). [Letter to J. Robert Ashcroft]. Evangel University Archives, Betty Chase Archive Rooms, J. Robert Ashcroft files and correspondence, Springfield, MO, United States.

Schreiner, L. A. (2018a). What Good Is Christian Higher Education? *Christian Higher Education*, *17*(1–2), 33–49. https://doi.org/10.1080/15363759.2018.1404362

Schreiner, L. A. (2018b). What Good Is Christian Higher Education? *Christian Higher Education*, *17*(1–2), 33–49. https://doi.org/10.1080/15363759.2018.1404362

Scott, C. W. H. (1955, September 8). [Charge of the President transcription]. Evangel University Archives, Betty Chase Archive Rooms, Klaude Kendrick Files, Springfield, MO, United States.

Scott, C. W. H. (1963, February 19). [Transcribed Oral History]. Evangel University Archives, Betty Chase Archive Rooms, Barry Corey Files, Springfield, MO, United States.

Spence, R. H. (1963, June 6). [Letter to J. Robert Ashcroft]. Evangel University Archives, Betty Chase Archive Rooms, J. Robert Ashcroft files, Springfield, MO, United States.

Spence, R. H. (1974, August 21). [Letter to J. Robert Ashcroft]. Evangel University Archives, Betty Chase Archive Rooms, J. Robert Ashcroft files, Springfield, MO, United States.

Spence, R. H. (1977, February 1). [Letter to all faculty and staff]. Evangel University

Archives, Betty Chase Archive Rooms, Robert H. Spence files, Springfield, MO, United States.

Spence, R. H. (2005). Interview by Betty Chase [Transcript]. Evangel University Archives, Betty Chase Archive Rooms, Springfield, MO, United States.

Stair, D. (2014). *History of Evangel University Athletics and Physical Education*. Springfield, MO.

Strahan, R. D. (1955). *A study to introduce curriculum approaches and student personnel services for Evangel College* (Evangel Kendrick Archives). http://0-search.ebscohost.com.swan.searchmobius.org/login.aspx?direct=true&db=cat07720a&AN=eul.b2660062&site=eds-live

[Survey of Practices]. (1968, September). Evangel University Archives, Betty Chase

Archive Rooms, J. Robert Ashcroft files, Springfield, MO, United States.

The College Curriculum. (1955, September 8). [Inauguration Program]. Evangel University Archives, Betty Chase Archive Rooms, Klaude Kendrick Files, Springfield, MO, United States.

The Holy Bible, NIV. (2011). Zondervan.

Title IX and Sex Discrimination. (2021, August 20). [Policy Guidance]. US Department of Education (ED). https://www2.ed.gov/about/offices/list/ocr/docs/tix_dis.html

Vygotsky, L. (1978). *Mind in Society*. Harvard University Press.

Vygotsky, L. s. (2020). *Educational Psychology*. CRC Press. https://doi.org/10.4324/9780429273070

Williams, W. R. (1988, June 24). Interview by Betty Chase [Transcript]. Evangel

University Archives, Betty Chase Archive Rooms, Barry Corey Files, Springfield, MO, United States.

Winehouse, I. (1959). *The Assemblies of God: A Popular Survey*. (Betty Chase Archive Rooms, Klaude Kendrick Library, Evangel University). Gospel Publishing House

Wolterstorff, N., Stronks, G. G., & Joldersma, C. W. (2002). *Educating for life: Reflections on Christian teaching and learning* (Evangel AGTS General Circulation). Baker Academic.

Woodhouse, K. (2015, September 28). *Closures to Triple*. Inside Higher Ed. https://www.insidehighered.com/news/2015/09/28/moodys-predicts-college-closures-triple-2017

Yeon Choi, & Mai-Dalton, R. R. (1999). The model of followers' responses to self-sacrificial leadership: An empirical test. *Leadership Quarterly*, *10*(3), 397. https://doi.org/10.1016/S1048-9843(99)00025-9

Yong, A. (2021). Theological Education between the West and the "Rest": A Reverse "Reverse Missionary" and Pentecost Perspective. *Asian Journal of Pentecostal Studies*, *24*(1), 21–37.

Zimmerman, T. F. (1973, August 29). [Letter to J. Robert Ashcroft on behalf of General Presbytery]. Evangel University Archives, Betty Chase Archive Rooms, J. Robert Ashcroft files, Springfield, MO, United States.

Zimmerman, T. F. (1988, February 22). Interview by Betty Chase [Transcript]. Evangel University Archives, Betty Chase Archive Rooms, Barry Corey Files, Springfield, MO, United States.

Appendices

Appendix A
Registrar's Enrollment Report for 1955 – 1980
SUMMARY OF ENROLLMENTS

	Fall		Spring		Summer			
Year	New TUG	New + Returning	New TUG	New + Returning	New TUG	New + Returning	Total New for Year	Unduplicated
1955-56	93	93	13	91	0	0	106	106
1956-57	100	183	0	195	0	0	100	183
1957-58	156	288	36	274	0	0	192	324
1958-59	215	405	61	403	0	0	276	466
1959-60	280	530	72	497	0	0	352	602
1960-61	292	558	46	533	0	0	338	604
1961-62	285	568	55	541	0	0	340	623
1962-63	272	589	56	547	0	0	328	645
1963-64	324	615	60	588	0	0	384	675
1964-65	350	719	68	683	0	0	418	787
1965-66	346	761	50	712	0	0	396	811
1966-67	369	822	49	780	0	0	418	871
1967-68	349	872	50	773	11	166	410	933
1968-69	334	881	46	833	11	210	391	938
1969-70	374	977	50	941	5	226	429	1032
1970-71	466	1120	44	1028	0	0	510	1164
1971-72	512	1228	58	1165	0	0	570	1286
1972-73	451	1219	53	1120	4	177	508	1276
1973-74	427	1142	71	1084	6	193	504	1219
1974-75	431	1165	74	1091	8	172	513	1247
1975-76	421	1133	63	1091	29	160	513	1225
1976-77	420	1126	104	1111	13	247	537	1243
1977-78	597	1291	101	1203	12	206	710	1404
1978-79	693	1460	133	1418	12	102	838	1605
1979-80	659	1612	104	1571	15	357	778	1731
1980-81	760	1851	154	1785	26	334	940	2031

Appendix B
In-person Guiding Interview Questions

- Where are you from originally?
- How did you hear about Evangel?
- What drew you to attend Evangel?
- Was Evangel your first choice?
- Why/Why not? What other schools did you consider?
- Why did you choose Evangel?
- How did attending/working at Evangel impact your life?
- In your opinion, what makes the Evangel experience different from other university experiences? Top three ways?
- What are Evangel's strengths?
- What are Evangel's weaknesses?
- Did an Evangel faculty or staff member provide a meaningful, supportive relationship while you were at Evangel? If so, describe and explain why this was important to your development?
- "Finding your calling" is a big part of the Evangel experience, how has the idea of "finding your calling" played out in your life?
- How did your professors influence your understanding of calling? Integration of faith and learning?
- How did your professors and campus leaders incorporate the "Christian" element of your Christian University experience?
- During your time at Evangel, do you feel Evangel accomplished its mission?

Appendices

- What are some of your favorite memories of Evangel?
- In your opinion, what are the top accomplishments from your time at Evangel?
- Who are other leaders from your time you would recommend for an interview?

Appendix C

Email introduction and invitation for interview

Greetings,

I have begun pursuing my doctorate degree through the EDD program here at Evangel, and part of my research includes interviewing members of the Evangel community who can provide perspective from 1955-1980. I'd like to conduct research on the first 25 years of the university and explore the forming of the ethos of Evangel which includes the integration of faith and learning as well as the idea that we are all called. If you are familiar with the dissertation completed by Dr. Barry Corey, my goal is to pick up where he left off.

If you are up for it, I would love to spend some time interviewing you to explore these topics. I would send a list of questions beforehand to guide our conversation with the flexibility that we may dig into related topics as well.

Is that something you would be open to doing?

Thank you for your time!

Hector Cruz '09 & '13, CFRE

Appendix D

Mass Survey Student Experience Survey Questions

1. How did you first learn about Evangel
    a. Parents
    b. Lead Pastor
    c. Youth Pastor
    d. Other Church Member
    e. AG Publication (Pentecostal Evangel, CA Herald, etc.)
    f. Evangel Student
    g. Evangel Administrator, Faculty, or Staff Member
    h. Representatives from the university (music group, sports team, etc.)
    i. Other (please share)
2. What was your academic major?
3. What years did you attend Evangel?
4. Did you graduate from Evangel?
    a. Yes
    b. No
5. What year did you graduate or what was your last year of attendance?
6. What are your top 2-3 memories or experiences from your time as a student?
7. Evangel University has been successful in perpetuating the Pentecostal tradition of the Assemblies of God.
    a. Strongly agree
    b. Somewhat agree
    c. Neither agree nor disagree
    d. Somewhat disagree
    e. Strongly disagree

8. Evangel University has provided higher education for students who were called in areas outside of vocational church ministry (ministers and missionaries.
    a. Strongly agree
    b. Somewhat agree
    c. Neither agree nor disagree
    d. Somewhat disagree
    e. Strongly disagree
9. The university mission should include perpetuating the Assemblies of God as a fellowship or denomination.
    a. Strongly agree
    b. Somewhat agree
    c. Neither agree nor disagree
    d. Somewhat disagree
    e. Strongly disagree
10. In your experience while you were a student, what were Evangel's strengths?
11. In your experience while you were a student, what were Evangel's weaknesses?
12. What was your church affiliation prior to your time as a student at Evangel?
    a. Assemblies of God
    b. Baptist
    c. Christian & Missionary Alliance (CMA)
    d. Church of Christ
    e. Church of God
    f. Evangelical Free
    g. Lutheran
    h. Methodist

- i. Nazarene
- j. Non-denominational
- k. Other (Please share)

13. What was your church affiliation immediately following your time at Evangel?
    - a. Assemblies of God
    - b. Baptist
    - c. Christian & Missionary Alliance (CMA)
    - d. Church of Christ
    - e. Church of God
    - f. Evangelical Free
    - g. Lutheran
    - h. Methodist
    - i. Nazarene
    - j. Non-denominational
    - k. Other (Please share)

14. What is your church affiliation today?
    - a. Assemblies of God
    - b. Baptist
    - c. Christian & Missionary Alliance (CMA)
    - d. Church of Christ
    - e. Church of God
    - f. Evangelical Free
    - g. Lutheran
    - h. Methodist
    - i. Nazarene
    - j. Non-denominational
    - k. Other (Please share)

15. In your opinion, what are the distinctive qualities of the Assemblies of God belief system?
16. Please list the names of faculty or staff members who positively contributed to your experience at Evangel and how they did so.
17. While a student at Evangel, what was the biggest influence on your spiritual growth? (Please check all that apply)
    a. Yourself
    b. Parents
    c. Siblings
    d. Friends
    e. Church Pastor
    f. Campus Pastor
    g. Professor
    h. Other School Staff
    i. Someone else (Please share)
18. Please rate the following statements based on a scale of 1 to 10 (1 being the minimum and 10 being the maximum).
    a. My Evangel experience contributed to my spiritual formation and development.
    b. My Evangel experienced contributed to my understanding of calling.
    c. My Evangel experience strengthened my faith in Jesus Christ.
    d. My Evangel experience encouraged me to take personal responsibility for my own spiritual growth.

e. My Evangel experience revealed teachers/faculty who modeled and reinforced how to grow spiritually.
f. My Evangel experience prepared me for my career.
g. My Evangel experience included adequate academic preparation in the classroom.
h. My Evangel experience provided meaningful relationships which impacted my life.

19. There have been several documented reports of revivals occurring on campus during the first 25 years of the university's experience. If you had firsthand experience with one of these revivals, please share what you remember from that experience (how it began, where it happened, who was involved, etc.)?

20. How important were each of the following in helping you decide to attend Evangel? (1 being Not important at all and 10 being Extremely Important)
    a. Accreditation
    b. Financial Aid
    c. Addiliation with the Assemblies of God
    d. Family and friends who attended
    e. President of the University
    f. Faculty/Professor
    g. Academic Major offered
    h. Athletics (please share what sport)
    i. Referral (please share by whom)

21. What else would you like to share about your experience at Evangel that will increase our understanding of its culture and impact on your life during your time as a student?
22. What is your gender?
23. Where are you originally from prior to attending Evangel?
24. Approximately what size town did you live in prior to attending Evangel?
    a. 1-25,000 people
    b. 25,001-50,000 people
    c. 50,001-100,000 people
    d. 100,001-250,000 people
    e. 250,000+ people

Appendix E
Survey Invitation Emails

Email #1

Dear Fellow Evangel Alum,

My name is Hector Cruz, and I am currently pursuing a Doctorate in Educational Leadership through the Evangel University Education department. I am researching the first 25 years of existence of Evangel, 1955 – 1980. If you are familiar with the work of Dr. Barry Corey, I am attempting to build on his historical narrative which focuses on the founding of Evangel from 1914-1955. The title of my dissertation is A HISTORICAL NARRATIVE AND STUDENT EXPERIENCE ANALYSIS OF THE FIRST TWENTY-FIVE YEARS OF EVANGEL UNIVERSITY. I am compiling a historical narrative based on archival historical documents, recorded oral histories and alumni interviews, and feedback to surveys, like the one I am asking you to complete in this email. Will you help establish this important historical narrative by sharing your responses to the survey linked here?

Take Survey HERE!

Your participation in this research is voluntary, and you can decline or stop completing the survey at any time. All responses will be used for research related to this study and historical narrative. Your responses will be anonymous, and all data collected during the study will be kept on a password-protected computer for five years and then destroyed, per research policy. The length of time it takes to complete the survey will be determined by the amount of information you provide as several questions are open-ended. If you are comfortable sharing your responses to this survey,

Pioneering Spirit

I would ask that you complete the survey only once with complete honesty. If you and your spouse are both alumni from the time period I am studying, I would ask you each to respond individually to the survey. You do not need to have graduated in order to complete the survey. I would also ask that you submit the survey by February 15, 2023 to allow me time to compile the survey results and findings.

Thank you for your consideration, and please let me know if you have any questions. You can reach me directly at CruzH@evangel.edu.

Thank you!

Hector Cruz '09 & '13, CFRE

Email #2

Dear Fellow Evangel Alum,

This is simply a reminder of the invitation to complete an important survey sharing your experience as a student at Evangel. If you have already completed and submitted the survey, THANK YOU! You do not need to complete it again. One note, at the bottom of the survey page, there are small arrows that serve as the SUBMIT button. When you are finished with the survey, click those arrows and your survey responses will be submitted.

My name is Hector Cruz, and I am currently pursuing a Doctorate in Educational Leadership through the Evangel University Education department. I am researching the first 25 years of existence of Evangel, 1955 – 1980. If you are familiar with the work of Dr. Barry Corey, I am attempting to build on his historical narrative which focuses on the founding of Evangel from 1914-1955. The title of my dissertation is A HISTORICAL NARRATIVE AND STUDENT EXPERIENCE ANALYSIS

OF THE FIRST TWENTY-FIVE YEARS OF EVANGEL UNIVERSITY. I am compiling a historical narrative based on archival historical documents, recorded oral histories and alumni interviews, and feedback to surveys, like the one I am asking you to complete in this email. Will you help establish this important historical narrative by sharing your responses to the survey linked here?

Take Survey HERE!

Your participation in this research is voluntary, and you can decline or stop completing the survey at any time. All responses will be used for research related to this study and historical narrative. Your responses will be anonymous, and all data collected during the study will be kept on a password-protected computer for five years and then destroyed, per research policy. The length of time it takes to complete the survey will be determined by the amount of information you provide as several questions are open-ended. If you are comfortable sharing your responses to this survey, I would ask that you complete the survey only once with complete honesty. If you and your spouse are both alumni from the time period I am studying, I would ask you each to respond individually to the survey. You do not need to have graduated in order to complete the survey. I would also ask that you submit the survey by February 15, 2023 to allow me time to compile the survey results and findings.

Thank you for your consideration, and please let me know if you have any questions. You can reach me directly at CruzH@evangel.edu.

Thank you!

Hector Cruz '09 & '13, CFRE

Email #3

Dear Fellow Evangel Alum,

This is simply a reminder of the invitation to complete an important survey sharing your experience as a student at Evangel. If you have already completed and submitted the survey, THANK YOU! You do not need to complete it again. We recently adjusted our email system so I'm hopeful this will reach more alumni. However, if you know of someone who should also complete the survey, please feel free to forward it to them as well.

One note, at the bottom of the survey page, there are small arrows that serve as the SUBMIT button. When you are finished with the survey, click those arrows and your survey responses will be submitted.

My name is Hector Cruz, and I am currently pursuing a Doctorate in Educational Leadership through the Evangel University Education department. I am researching the first 25 years of existence of Evangel, 1955 – 1980. If you are familiar with the work of Dr. Barry Corey, I am attempting to build on his historical narrative which focuses on the founding of Evangel from 1914-1955. The title of my dissertation is A HISTORICAL NARRATIVE AND STUDENT EXPERIENCE ANALYSIS OF THE FIRST TWENTY-FIVE YEARS OF EVANGEL UNIVERSITY. I am compiling a historical narrative based on archival historical documents, recorded oral histories and alumni interviews, and feedback to surveys, like the one I am asking you to complete in this email. Will you help establish this important historical narrative by sharing your responses to the survey linked here?

Appendices

Take Survey HERE!

Your participation in this research is voluntary, and you can decline or stop completing the survey at any time. All responses will be used for research related to this study and historical narrative. Your responses will be anonymous, and all data collected during the study will be kept on a password-protected computer for five years and then destroyed, per research policy. The length of time it takes to complete the survey will be determined by the amount of information you provide as several questions are open-ended. If you are comfortable sharing your responses to this survey, I would ask that you complete the survey only once with complete honesty. If you and your spouse are both alumni from the time period I am studying, I would ask you each to respond individually to the survey. You do not need to have graduated in order to complete the survey. I would also ask that you submit the survey by February 15, 2023 to allow me time to compile the survey results and findings.

Thank you for your consideration, and please let me know if you have any questions. You can reach me directly at CruzH@evangel.edu.

Thank you!

Hector Cruz '09 & '13, CFRE

Appendix F
Data Analysis and Triangulation Examples

Data Analysis Examples				
Material References	Historical Documents	Interviews	Surveys	Major Theme
Barracks	Archival Photos, Campus Development Documents, Oral Histories and Transcripts	The Barracks were discussed in every interview.	Referenced 55 times	Shared Experiences
Spiritual Formation	Presidential Speech Transcripts, Faculty Meeting Minutes and Notes	Several included quotes reveal how this was a core experience.	Figure 20, 23, 27, 28, 29	Shared Experiences/Founding Mission Fulfilled
Academics	Accreditation Reports, Faculty Meeting Minutes and Notes	Careers and titles of interviewees revealed how prepared and equipped they were.	Figure 21, 24	Shared Experiences/Founding Mission Fulfilled
Impact of Faculty and Leaders	Presidential Letters and Communication, Faculty and Leader Oral Histories and Transcripts	Every interviewee was asked for names of faculty and leaders who impacted them as students.	Figure 25, Open ended survey responses referencing professors and administrators	Self-Sacrificial Leadership
Presidential Leadership and Transitions	Letters of Resignation, Presidential Communication, Oral Histories and Transcripts	Interviewees did not know details of transitions, but they spoke of meaningful relationships and respect for "their" president.	Figure 19, Open ended survey responses about presidential leadership and relationships	Political Awareness

Evangel History of Sport

	F	CC	MS	MBB	W	BB	MT	MTen	MG	WBB	WV	WTen	WT	S	FH
1955-56				X											
1956-57				X											
1957-58				X											
1958-59				X											
1959-60				X			X	X							
1960-61				X			X								
1961-62				X			X								
1962-63				X			X	X							
1963-64				X			X	X							
1964-65				X		X	X	X							
1965-66				X		X	X	X	X			X			
1966-67				X		X	X	X	X		X	X	X	X	
1967-68				X	X	X	X	X	X	X	X	X	X	X	
1968-69			X	X	X	X	X	X	X	X	X	X	X	X	X
1969-70		X	X	X	X	X	X	X	X	X	X	X	X	X	
1970-71		X	X	X	X	X	X	X	X	X	X	X	X	X	
1971-72		X	X	X	X	X	X	X	X	X	X	X			
1872-73		X	X	X	X	X	X	X	X	X	X	X			
1973-74		X	X	X		X	X	X	X	X	X	X			
1974-75		X		X		X	X	X	X	X	X	X			
1975-76		X		X		X			X	X	X	X			
1976-77				X		X		X		X	X	X	X		
1977-78	X			X		X		X	X	X	X	X	X		
1978-79	X			X		X		X	X	X	X	X	X		
1979-80	X	X		X		X		X		X	X	X	X		
1980-81	X	X		X		X		X	X	X	X	X	X		

Appendix G
History of Athletics – 1955-1980

F - Football
CC - Cross Country
MS - Men's Soccer
MBB - Men's Basketball
W - Wrestling
BB - Baseball
MT - Men's Track
MTen - Men's Tennis
MG - Men's Golf
WBB - Women's Basketball
WV - Women's Volleyball
WTen - Women's Tennis
WT - Women's Track
S - Softball
FH - Field Hockey

Appendix H

MINUTES FACULTY MEETING November 15, 1973
PURPOSE OF MEETING

This specially called faculty meeting followed the conclusion of the regular meeting of the Executive Presbytery of the Assemblies of God and was convened to report actions of the Presbytery concerning Evangel College. Members of the Executive Presbytery present to convey the sentiments and actions of the full body were General Superintendent Thomas F. Zimmerman, Assistant General Superintendent of Kansas), and the Rev. James Hamill (pastor, Memphis, Tennessee).

The General Superintendent provided a background review of past actions of the General Council in behalf of Evangel College and concluded his remarks by reading the following official actions of the Executive Presbytery:

A motion prevailed to adopt the following statement and to authorize its release: That in light of the unanimous statement of the General Presbytery to the effect that it totally identifies with the mission of Evangel College and feels that its operation is an essential part of the total ministry of the Assemblies of God, and in view of the need for undergirding the morale of all levels of college activity, the Executive Presbytery calls for the uniting of effort on the part of the total college community in presenting a solidarity of purpose and effort in stabilizing the spiritual, academic and economic program of the college; and further, that the Executive Presbytery assures every level of the college concerned of its total backing and support of every effort to not only solve the present need but to project a program for the future which will contribute to both student procurement and financial undergirdment.

Furthermore, a call is hereby made for a clear communication to be made to all levels of college activity that there is a compatible relationship existing between the movement, the Board and the college administration. It is requested that all levels pull together for the achieving of a common objective. In order for this to be communicated, it is authorized that representatives of the Executive Presbytery convey to the College Board of Directors, administration, faculty, staff and student body that there exists this very sensitive concern for the successful continuity of the college program. Furthermore, that an appeal be made to those presently responsible for the program of the college and its implementation, to hold steady in prayer and faith to see the program of the college successfully implemented in a responsible way.

A motion was duly adopted: That in view of the fact that Evangel College is a college of arts and sciences totally owned and operated by the Assemblies of God, we urge that it be communicated to all levels of the Assemblies of God constituency the proper place in Christian stewardship which should be given in prayer for, and in financial support of, operational needs of the college program and that we urge that Districts, churches and individuals, where possible, be requested to give on a regular monthly basis a sum of money undesignated so that a base of continuing support will be provided for this approved operation; and that we urge the administration to use this plea for support in mounting a program of solicitation which will provide a program for the support of Evangel College.

After informal expressions of appreciation from the other three members of the Executive Presbytery present, it was

MSP to express the appreciation of the entire college family for the re-affirmation and re-articulation of support for Evangel College by all administrative levels of the General Council of the Assemblies of God.

As a tangible expression of the sentiment of the Executive Presbytery, a personal check was presented to President Ashcroft. Other personal commitments were made by Presbytery members and will be forthcoming.

The meeting was concluded with prayer by Rev. James Hamill.

Respectfully submitted, Zenas J. Bicket

Interim Dean

ZJB/1t

Appendix I
INFORMED CONSENT LETTER

- I voluntarily agree to participate in this research study.
- I understand that even if I agree to participate now, I can withdraw at any time or refuse to answer any question without any consequences of any kind.
- I understand that I can withdraw permission to use data from my interview within two weeks after the interview, in which case the material will be deleted.
- I have had the purpose and nature of the study explained to me in writing and I have had the opportunity to ask questions about the study.
- I understand that participation involves an interview with the researcher to discuss my experience, perspective, perceptions, and opinions related to my time at Evangel University between 1955 and 1980.
- I understand that I will not benefit directly from participating in this research.
- I agree to my interview being audio-recorded.
- I understand that all information I provide for this study will be treated confidentially.
- I understand that in any report on the results of this research my identity will remain anonymous. This will be done by changing or redacting my name and disguising any details of my interview which may reveal my identity.
- I understand that disguised extracts from my interview may be quoted in the researcher's dissertation, presentations, or future published works.
- I understand that signed consent forms and original

audio recordings will be retained in secure possession of the researcher until the dissertation defense is approved.
- I understand that a transcript of my interview will be retained for one year after the dissertation defense is approved.
- I understand that under freedom of information legislation I am entitled to access the information I have provided at any time while it is in storage as specified above.
- I understand that I am free to contact any of the people involved in the research to seek further clarification and information.

Hector L. Cruz

Bachelor of Business Administration in Management

Evangel University

Master of Organizational Leadership

Evangel University

417.865.2815 ext. 7345

CruzH@evangel.edu

1111 N Glenstone Ave

Springfield, MO 65802

———————————————

Signature of participant and date

I believe the participant is giving informed consent to participate in this study

———————————————

Signature of researcher and date

About the Author

Hector Cruz was born near Miami, Florida, where the Puerto Rican half of him enjoyed plenty of rice and beans. He attended high school in Hamburg, Pennsylvania, where the German half of him enjoyed plenty of mashed potatoes and sauerkraut. He went on to attend Evangel University, where he earned a BBA in Management, a Master's in Organizational Leadership, and an EdD in Educational Leadership. As a student at Evangel, he met his beautiful wife and then spent fifteen years working at the University in a variety of roles. He and his wife have three incredible children and count their blessings daily.

You can learn more about Hector and contact him at his website www.daddylessonsblog.com.